HOCKEY RULES ILLUSTRATED

HOCKEY RULES ILLUSTRATED

Edited by George Sullivan

Produced and designed by
Howard Petlack, A Good Thing, Inc.

A FIRESIDE BOOK

PUBLISHED BY SIMON & SCHUSTER, INC.
NEW YORK

Photography by Manhattan Image, N.Y., N.Y.

Special Thanks to
Tom "Boom Boom" Klavans and
Dan "The Slammer" Klotz

National Hockey League photos by Bruce Bennett

The official rules of the
National Hockey League are reprinted by the permission of the
National Hockey League.

First Fireside Edition, 1986

Published by Simon & Schuster, Inc.
Simon & Schuster Building
Rockefeller Center
1230 Avenue of the Americas
New York, New York 10020

FIRESIDE and colophon are registered trademarks of Simon & Schuster, Inc.

Manufactured in the United States of America

10   9   8   7   6   5   4   3   2   1

Library of Congress Cataloging in Publication Data

ISBN: 0-671-63585-9

Contents

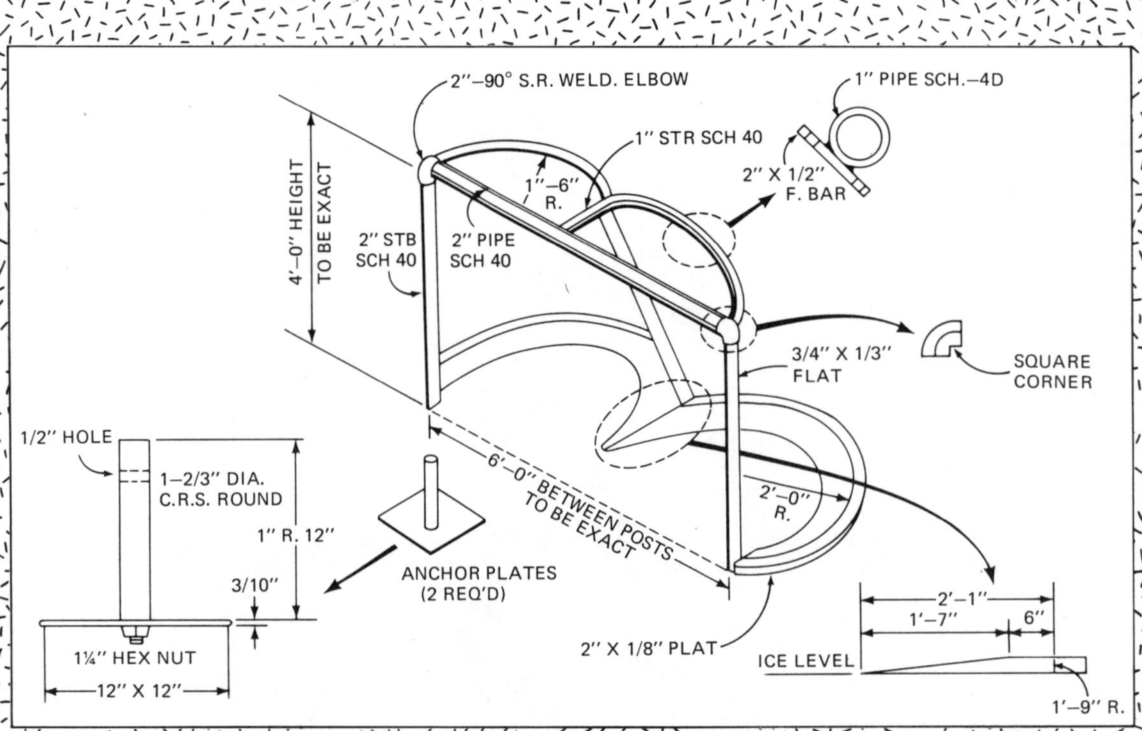

2"—90° S.R. WELD. ELBOW
1" PIPE SCH.—4D
1" STR SCH 40
2" X 1/2" F. BAR
4'-0" HEIGHT TO BE EXACT
1"—6" R.
2" STB SCH 40
2" PIPE SCH 40
3/4" X 1/3" FLAT
SQUARE CORNER
1/2" HOLE
1—2/3" DIA. C.R.S. ROUND
1" R. 12"
3/10"
6'-0" BETWEEN POSTS TO BE EXACT
2'-0" R.
ANCHOR PLATES (2 REQ'D)
1¼" HEX NUT
12" X 12"
2" X 1/8" PLAT
ICE LEVEL
2'-1"
1'-7"
6"
1'-9" R.

Rule 1 / Rink

The game of "Ice Hockey" shall be played on an ice surface known as a "RINK".

NOTE *There shall be no markings on the ice except as provided under these rules without the express written permission of the League.*

Rule 2 / Dimensions of Rink

a The official size of the rink shall be two hundred feet long and eighty-five feet wide. The corners shall be rounded in the arc of a circle with radius of twenty-eight feet.

The rink shall be surrounded by a wooden or fiberglass wall or fence known as the "boards" which shall extend not less than forty inches and not more than forty-eight inches above the level of the ice surface. The ideal height of the boards above the ice surface shall be forty-two inches. Except for the official markings provided for in these rules the entire playing surface and the boards shall be white in color except the kick plate at the bottom of the board which shall be light blue or light yellow in color.

Any variations from any of the foregoing dimensions shall require official authorization by the League.

b The boards shall be constructed in such manner that the surface facing the ice shall be smooth and free of any obstruction or any object that could cause injury to players.

All doors giving access to the playing surface must swing away from the ice surface.

All glass, wire or other types of protective screens and gear used to hold them in position shall be mounted on the boards on the side away from the playing surface.

Rule 3 / Goal Posts and Nets

a Ten feet from each end of the rink and in the center of a red line two inches wide, drawn completely across the width of the ice and continued vertically up the side of the boards, regulation goal posts and nets shall be set in such manner as to remain stationary during the progress of a game. The goal posts shall be kept in position by means of metal rods or pipes affixed in the ice or floor and projecting a minimum of eight inches above the ice surface.

Where the length of the playing surface exceeds two hundred feet the goal line and goal posts may be placed not more than fifteen feet from the end of the rink.

b The goal posts shall be of approved design and material, extending vertically four feet above the surface of the ice and set six feet apart measured from the inside of the posts. A cross bar of the same material as the goal posts shall extend from the top of one post to the top of the other.

NOTE *For League games the "NHL Official Goal Frame and Net" are approved and adopted. The design and specifications set out in the Plan of Goal printed in this Rule Book are official.*

c There shall be attached to each goal frame a net of approved design made of white nylon cord which shall be draped in such a manner as to prevent the puck coming to rest on the outside of it.

A skirt of heavy white nylon fabric or heavyweight white canvas shall be laced around the

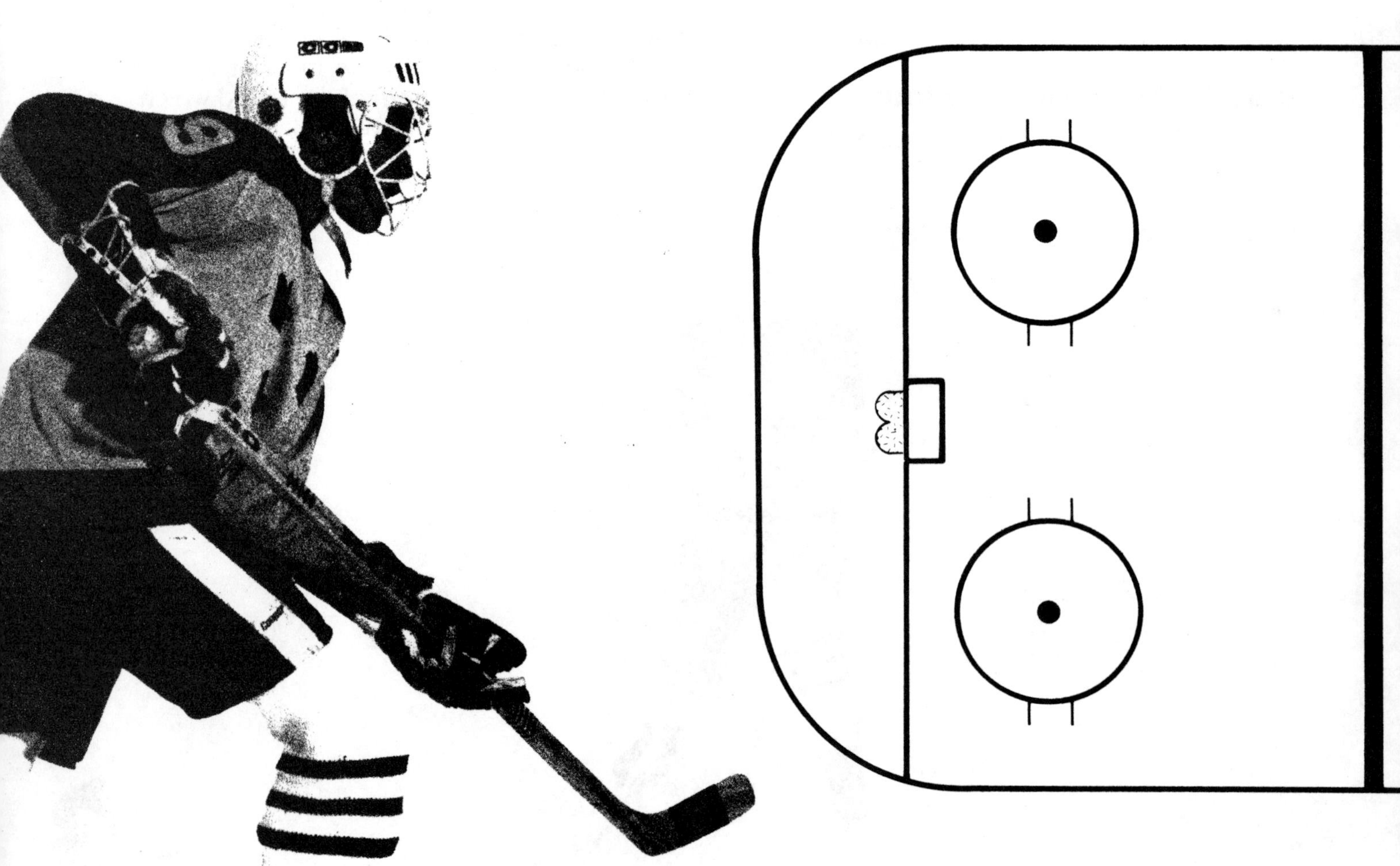

"3" base plate of the goal frame in such a way as to protect the net from being cut or broken. This skirt shall not project more than one inch above the base plate.

NOTE *The frame of the goal including the small "3" attached to the top crossbar shall be draped with a nylon mesh net so as to completely enclose the back of the frame. The net shall be made of three-ply twisted twine (0.130 inch diameter) or equivalent braided twine of multifilament white nylon with an appropriate tensile strength of 700 pounds. The size of the mesh shall be two and one-half inches (inside measurement) from each knot to each diagonal knot when fully stretched. Knotting shall be made so as to ensure no sliding of the twine. The net shall be laced to the frame with medium white nylon cord no smaller in size than #21.*

d The goal posts and cross bar shall be painted in red and all other exterior surfaces shall be painted in white.

e The red line, two inches wide, between the goal posts on the ice and extended completely across the rink, shall be known as the "GOAL LINE".

f The Goal area, enclosed by the goal line and the base of the goal, shall be painted white.

Rule 4 / Goal Crease

a In front of each goal a "GOAL CREASE" area shall be marked by a red line two inches in width.

b The goal crease shall be laid out as follows: One foot from the outside of each goal post, lines four feet in length and two inches in width shall be drawn at right angles to the goal line and the points of these lines farthest from the goal line shall be joined by another line, two inches in width.

c The goal crease area shall include all the space outlined by the crease lines and extending vertically four feet to the level of the top of the goal frame.

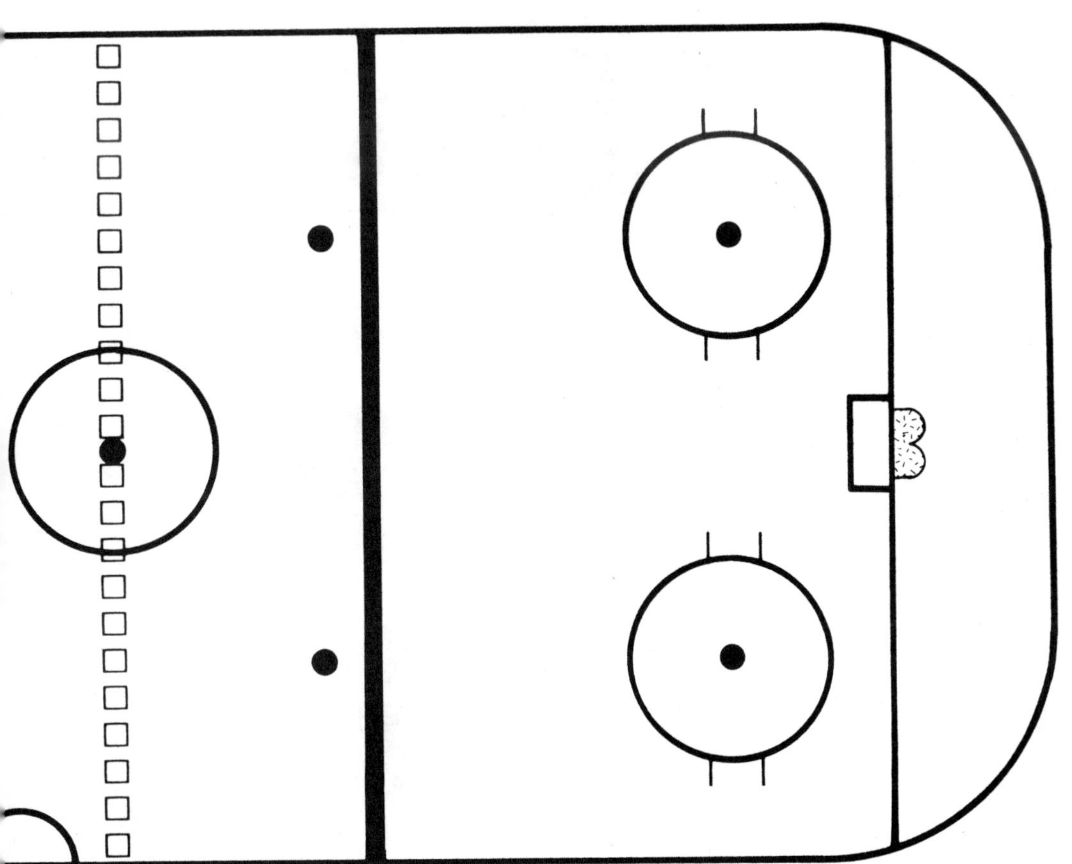

9

Rule 5 / Division of Ice Surface

a The ice area between the two goals shall be divided into three parts by lines, twelve inches in width, and blue in color, drawn sixty feet out from the goal lines, and extended completely across the rink, parallel with the goal lines, and continued vertically up the side of boards.

b That portion of the ice surface in which the goal is situated shall be called the "DEFEND-ING ZONE" of the team defending that goal; the central portion shall be known as the "NEU-TRAL ZONE", and the portion farthest from the defended goal as the "ATTACKING ZONE".

c There shall also be a line, twelve inches in width, and red in color, drawn completely across the rink in center ice, parallel with the goal lines and continued vertically up the side of the boards, known as the "CENTER LINE". This line shall contain at regular intervals mark-ings of a uniform distinctive design which will easily distinguish it from the two blue lines . . . the outer edges of which must be continuous.

Rule 6 / Center Ice Spot and Circle

A circular blue spot, twelve inches in diameter, shall be marked exactly in the center of the rink: and with this spot as a center a circle of fifteen feet radius shall be marked with a blue line two inches in width.

Rule 7 / Face-off Spots in Neutral Zone

Two red spots two feet in diameter shall be marked on the ice in the Neutral Zone five feet from each blue line. The spots shall be forty-four feet apart and each shall be a uniform dis-tance from the adjacent boards.

Rule 8 / End Zone Face-off Spots and Circles

a In both end zones and on both sides of each goal, red face-off spots and circles shall be marked on the ice. The face-off spots shall be two feet in diameter and extending from each end of the spot and parallel to the boards shall be marked a line six inches in length and two inches wide.

The circles shall be two inches wide with a radi-us of fifteen feet from the center of the face-off spots. At the outer edge of both sides of each face-off circle and parallel to the goal line shall be marked two red lines, two inches wide and two feet in length and three feet apart.

Parallel to the goal line and equidistant from and on opposite sides of the center of each end face-off spot two red lines six feet in length and three inches in width and six feet apart shall be marked on the ice. Perpendicular from the cen-ter of these lines and extending away from the center face-off circle is drawn a line three feet long and three inches wide. (The effect of these lines is to produce a 'T' on opposite sides of the center face-off spot.)

b The location of the face-off spots shall be fixed in the following manner:

Along a line twenty feet from each goal line and parallel to it, mark two points twenty-two feet on both sides of the straight line joining the centers of the two goals. Each such point shall be the center of a face-off spot and circle.

Rule 9 / Players' Bench

a Each rink shall be provided with seats or benches for the use of players of both teams and the accommodations provided including benches and doors shall be uniform for both teams. Such seats or benches shall have accommodation for at least fourteen persons of each team, and shall be placed immediately alongside the ice, in the Neutral Zone, as near to the center of the rink as possible with doors opening in the Neutral Zone and convenient to the dressing rooms.

Each players' bench should be twenty-four feet in length and when situated in the spectator area they shall be separated from the spectators by a protective glass of sufficient height so as to afford the necessary protection for the players. The players' benches shall be on the same side of the playing surface opposite the penalty bench and should be separated by a substantial distance.

NOTE *Those buildings that were built prior to the introduction of this Rule and in which players' benches were installed on opposite sides of the rink are exempt from this Rule.*

Where physicially possible each Players' Bench shall have two doors opening in the Neutral Zone and all doors opening to the playing surface shall be constructed so that they swing inward.

b None but players in uniform, Manager, Coach and Trainer shall be permitted to occupy the benches so provided.

Rule 10 / Penalty Bench

a Each rink must be provided with benches or seats to be known as the "PENALTY BENCH". These benches or seats must be capable of accommodating a total of ten persons including the Penalty Timekeepers. Separate penalty benches shall be provided for each team and they shall be situated on opposite sides of the Timekeeper's area. The penalty bench(es) must be situated in the Neutral Zone.

b On the ice immediatedly in front of the Penalty Timekeeper's seat there shall be marked in red on the ice a semi-circle of ten feet radius and two inches in width which shall be known as the "REFEREE'S CREASE".

12

c Each "Penalty Bench" shall be protected from the spectator area by means of a glass partition which shall be not less than five feet above the height of the boards.

Rule 11 / Signal and Timing Devices

a Each rink must be provided with a siren, or other suitable sound device, for the use of Timekeepers.

b Each rink shall be provided with some form of electrical clock for the purpose of keeping the spectators, players and game officials accurately informed as to all time elements at all stages of the game including the time remaining to be played in any period and the time remaining to be served by at least five penalized players on each team.

Time recording for both game time and penalty time shall show time remaining to be played or served.

c Behind each goal electrical lights shall be set up for the use of the Goal Judges. A red light will signify the scoring of a goal. Where automatic lights are available, a green light will signify the end of a period or a game.

NOTE *A goal cannot be scored when a green light is showing.*

Rule 12 / Police Protection

All clubs shall provide adequate police or other protection for all players and officials at all times.

The Referee shall report to the President any failure of this protection observed by him or reported to him with particulars of such failure.

ST.LOUIS
BLUES

OILERS

TORONTO
MAPLE
LEAFS

Rule 13 / Composition of Team

a A team shall be composed of six players, who shall be under contract to the club they represent.

b Each player and each goalkeeper listed in the line-up of each team shall wear an individual identifying number at least ten inches high on the back of his sweater and, in addition, each player and goalkeeper shall wear his surname in full, in block letters 3″ high, across the back of his sweater at shoulder height.

All players of each team shall be dressed uniformly in conformity with approved design and color of their helmets, sweaters, pants, stockings and boots. Any player or goalkeeper not complying with this provision shall not be permitted to participate in the game.

Each Member Club shall design and wear distinctive and contrasting uniforms for their home and road games, no parts of which shall be interchangeable except the pants.

Rule 14 / Captain of Team

a One Captain shall be appointed by each team, and he alone shall have the privilege of discussing with the Referee any questions relating to interpretation of rules which may arise during the progress of a game. He shall wear the letter "C", approximately three inches in height and in contrasting color, in a conspicuous position on the front of his sweater.

b The Referee and Official Scorer shall be advised prior to the start of each game, the name of the Captain of the team and the designated substitute.

c No goalkeepers shall be entitled to exercise the privilege of Captain.

d Only the Captain, when invited to do so by the Referee, shall have the privilege of discussing any point relating to the interpretation of rules. Any Captain or player who comes off the bench and makes any protest or intervention with the Officials for any purpose must be assessed a misconduct penalty in addition to a minor penalty under Rule 42 (b)—Abuse of Officials.

A complaint about a penalty is NOT a matter "relating to the interpretation of the rules" and a minor penalty shall be imposed against any Captain or other player making such a complaint.

e No playing Coach or playing Manager shall be permitted to act as Captain.

Rule 15 / Players in Uniform

a At the beginning of each game the Manager or Coach of each team shall list the players and goalkeepers who shall be eligible to play in the game. Not more than seventeen players, exclusive of goalkeepers, shall be permitted.

In play-offs seventeen players, exclusive of goalkeepers, shall be permitted.

In exhibition games eighteen players, exclusive of goalkeepers, shall be permitted.

b A list of names and numbers of all eligible players and goalkeepers must be handed to the Referee or Official Scorer before the game, and no change shall be permitted in the list or addition thereto shall be permitted after the commencement of the game.

c Each team shall be allowed one goalkeeper on the ice at one time. The goalkeeper may be removed and another "player" substituted. Such substitute shall not be permitted the privileges of the goalkeeper.

d Each team shall have on its bench, or on a chair immediately beside the bench, a substitute goalkeeper who shall at all times be fully dressed and equipped ready to play.

The substitute goalkeeper may enter the game at any time following a stoppage of play but no warm-up shall be permitted.

e Except when both goalkeepers are incapacitated, no player on the playing roster in that game shall be permitted to wear the equipment of the goalkeeper.

f In regular League and Play-off games if both listed goalkeepers are incapacitated, that team shall be entitled to dress and play any available goalkeeper who is eligible. No delay shall be permitted in taking his position in the goal, and he shall be permitted a two-minute warm-up. However, the warm-up is not permitted in the event a goalkeeper is substituted for a penalty shot.

NOTE *The two-minute warm-up for a substitute goalkeeper shall be limited to one warm-up per game per goalkeeper.*

g The Referee shall report to the President for disciplinary action any delay in making a substitution of goalkeepers.

WASHINGTON
capitals

JETS
WINNIPEG

NEW YORK
RANGERS

NY
ISLANDERS

Los Angeles
KINGS

NORDIQUES
QUÉBEC

Rule 16 / Starting Line-Up

a Prior to the start of the game, at the request of the Referee, the Manager or Coach of the visiting team is required to name the starting line-up to the Referee or the Official Scorer. At any time in the game at the request of the Referee, made to the Captain, the visiting team must place a playing line-up on the ice and promptly commence play.

b Prior to the start of the game the Manager or Coach of the home team, having been advised by the Official Scorer or the Referee the names of the starting line-up of the visiting team, shall name the starting line-up of the home team which information shall be conveyed by the Official Scorer or the Referee to the Coach of the visiting team.

c No change in the starting line-up of either team as given to the Referee or Official Scorer, or in the playing line-up on the ice, shall be made until the game is actually in progress. For an infraction of this rule a bench minor penalty shall be imposed upon the offending team, provided such infraction is called to the attention of the Referee before the second face-off in the first period takes place.

d Following the stoppage of play the visiting team shall promptly place a line-up on the ice ready for play and no substitution shall be made from that time until play has been resumed. The home team may then make any desired substitution which does not result in the delay of the game.

If there is any undue delay by either team in changing lines the Referee shall order the offending team or teams to take their positions immediately and not permit a line change.

NOTE *When a substitution has been made under the above rule no additional substitution may be made until play commences.*

e The Referee shall give the Visiting Team a reasonable amount of time to make their change after which he shall put up his hand to indicate that no further change shall be made by the Visiting Club. At this point, the Home Team may change immediately. Any attempt by the Visiting Team to make a change after the Referee's signal shall result in the assessment of a bench minor penalty for delay of game.

Rule 17 / Equalizing of Teams

DELETED

Rule 18 / Change of Players

a Players may be changed at any time from the players' bench, provided that the player or players leaving the ice shall always be at the players' bench and out of the play before any change is made.

A goalkeeper may be changed for another player at any time under the conditions set out in this section.

NOTE 1 *When a goalkeeper leaves his goal area and proceeds to his players' bench for the purpose of substituting another player, the rear Linesman shall be responsible to see that the substitution made is not illegal by reason of the premature departure of the substitute from the bench (before the goalkeeper is within ten feet of the bench). If the substitution is made prematurely, the Linesman shall stop the play immediately by blowing his whistle unless the non-offending team has possession of the puck in which event the stoppage will be delayed until the puck changes hands. There shall be no time penalty to the team making the premature substitution but the resulting face-off will take place on the center "face-off spot".*

NOTE 2 *The referee shall request that the public address announcer make the following announcement: "Play has been stopped due to premature entry of a player from the players' bench." If in the course of making a substitution the player entering the game plays the puck with his stick, skates or hands or who checks or makes any physical contact with an opposing player while the retiring player is actually on the ice then the infraction of "too many men on the ice" will be called.*

If in the course of a substitution either the player entering the play or the player retiring is struck by the puck accidentally the play will not be stopped and no penalty will be called.

b If by reason of insufficient playing time remaining, or by reason of penalties already im-

posed, a bench minor penalty is imposed for deliberate illegal substitution (too many men on the ice) which cannot be served in its entirety within the legal playing time, a penalty shot shall be awarded against the offending team.

c A player serving a penalty on the penalty bench, who is to be changed after the penalty has been served, must proceed at once by way of the ice and be at his own players' bench before any change can be made.

For any violation of this rule a bench minor penalty shall be imposed.

Rule 19 / Injured Players

a When a player, other than a goalkeeper, is injured or compelled to leave the ice during a game, he may retire from the game and be replaced by a substitute, but play must continue without the teams leaving the ice.

b If a goalkeeper sustains an injury or becomes ill he must be ready to resume play immediately or be replaced by a substitute goalkeeper and NO additional time shall be allowed by the referee for the purpose of enabling the injured or ill goalkeeper to resume his position. (See also Section (d).)

c The Referee shall report to the President for disciplinary action any delay in making a goalkeeper substitution.

The substitute goalkeeper shall be subject to the regular rules governing goalkeepers and shall be entitled to the same privileges.

d When a substitution for the regular goalkeeper has been made, such regular goalkeeper shall not resume his position until the first stoppage of play thereafter.

e If a penalized player has been injured he may proceed to the dressing room without the necessity of taking a seat on the penalty bench. If the injured player receives a minor penalty the penalized team shall immediately put a substitute player without change. If the injured player receives a major penalty the penalized team shall place a substitute player on the penalty bench before the penalty expires and no other replacement for the penalized player shall be permitted to enter the game except from the penalty bench. For violation of this rule a bench minor penalty shall be imposed.

The penalized player who has been injured and been replaced on the penalty bench shall not be eligible to play until his penalty has expired.

f When a player is injured so that he cannot continue play or go to his bench, the play shall not be stopped until the injured player's team has secured possession of the puck; if the player's team is in possession of the puck at the time of injury, play shall be stopped immediately, unless his team is in a scoring position.

NOTE *In the case where it is obvious that a player has sustained a serious injury the Referee and/or Linesman may stop the play immediately.*

Rule 20 / Sticks

a The sticks shall be made of wood or other material approved by the Rules Committee, and must not have any projections. Adhesive tape of any color may be wrapped around the stick at any place for the purpose of reinforcement or to improve control of the puck. In the case of a goalkeeper's stick, there shall be a knob of white tape or some other protective material approved by the League not less than one-half inch ($1/2''$) thick at the top of the shaft.

b No stick shall exceed fifty-eight inches (58″) in length from heel to the end of the shaft nor more than twelve and one-half inches ($12 1/2''$) from the heel to the end of the blade.

The blade of the stick shall not be more than three inches in width at any point nor less than two inches. All edges of the blade shall be bevelled. The curvature of the blade of the stick shall be restricted in such a way that the distance of a perpendicular line measured from a straight line drawn from any point at the heel to the end of the blade to the point of maximum curvature shall not exceed one-half inch.

c The blade of the goalkeeper's stick shall not exceed three and one-half inches in width at any point except at the heel where it must not exceed four and one-half inches in width; nor shall the goalkeeper's stick exceed fifteen and one-half inches in length from the heel to the end of the blade.

The widened portion of the goalkeeper's stick extending up the shaft from the blade shall not extend more than twenty-six inches from the heel and shall not exceed three and one-half inches in width.

d A minor penalty plus a fine of two hundred dollars ($200.00) shall be imposed on any player or goalkeeper who uses a stick not conforming to the provisions of this rule.

NOTE 1 *When a formal complaint is made by the Captain or designated substitute of a team, against the dimensions of any stick, the Referee shall take the stick to the Timekeeper's bench where the necessary measurement shall be made immediately. The result shall be reported to the Penalty Timekeeper who shall record it on the back of the penalty record.*

If the complaint is not sustained a bench minor penalty shall be imposed against the complaining Club in addition to a fine of $100.

NOTE 2 *A player who participates in the play while taking a replacement stick to his goalkeeper shall incur a minor penalty under this rule but the automatic fine of two hundred dollars ($200.00) shall not be imposed. If his participation causes a foul resulting in a minor or major penalty the referee shall report the incident to the President for disciplinary action.*

e In the event that a player scores on a penalty shot while using an illegal stick the goal shall be disallowed and no further penalty imposed. However, if no goal is scored the player taking the penalty shot shall receive a minor penalty.

f A minor penalty plus a ten-minute misconduct penalty shall be imposed on any player who refuses to surrender his stick for measurement when requested to do so by the Referee. In addition this player shall be subject to a $200 fine.

Rule 21 / Skates

a All hockey skates shall be of a design approved by the Rules Committee. All skates worn by players (but not goalkeepers) and by the Referee and Linesmen shall be equipped with approved safety heel tips.

When the Referee becomes aware that any person is wearing a skate on which the protective heel tip is missing or broken, he shall direct its replacement at the next intermission. If such replacement is not carried out, the Referee shall report the incident to the President for disciplinary action.

b The use of speed skates or fancy skates or any skate so designed that it may cause injury is prohibited.

KOHO 2230
KOHO

Rule 22 / Goalkeeper's Equipment

a With the exception of skates and stick, all the equipment worn by the goalkeeper must be constructed solely for the purpose of protecting the head or body, and he must not wear any garment or use any contrivance which would give him undue assistance in keeping goal.

NOTE *Cages on gloves and abdominal aprons extending down the front of the thighs on the outside of the pants are prohibited. "Cage" shall mean any lacing or webbing or other material in the goalkeeper's glove joining the thumb and index finger which is in excess of the minimum necessary to fill the gap when the goalkeeper's thumb and forefinger in the glove are fully extended and spread and includes any pocket or pouch effect produced by excess lacing or webbing or other material between the thumb and forefinger when fully extended or spread.*

Protective padding attached to the back or forming part of goalkeeper's gloves shall not exceed eight inches in width nor more than sixteen inches in length at any point.

b The leg guards worn by goalkeepers shall not exceed ten inches in extreme width when on the leg of the player.

NOTE *At the commencement of each season and prior to play-offs goalkeepers' leg guards shall be checked by League Staff and* any violation of this rule shall be reported to the Club involved and to the President of the League.

c Protective masks of a design approved by the Rules Committee may be worn by goalkeepers.

Rule 23 / Protective Equipment

a All protective equipment, except gloves, headgear and goalkeepers' leg guards must be worn under the uniform. For violation of this rule, after warning by the Referee, a minor penalty shall be imposed.

NOTE *Players including the goalkeeper violating this rule shall not be permitted to participate in game until such equipment has been corrected or removed.*

b All players of both teams shall wear a helmet of design, material and construction approved by the Rules Committee at all times while participating in a game, either on the playing surface or the players' or penalty benches.

Players, who have been under Standard Player's contract to a Member Club of the League, at any time prior to June 1, 1979 may elect for exemption from the operation of this sub-section (b) by execution of an approved Request and Release form and filing it with the League office.

Rule 24 / Dangerous Equipment

a The use of pads or protectors made of metal, or of any other material likely to cause injury to a player, is prohibited.

b A mask or protector of a design approved by the Rules Committee may be worn by a player who has sustained a facial injury.

NOTE *All elbow pads which do not have a soft protective outer covering of sponge rubber or similar material at least 1/2 inch thick shall be considered dangerous equipment.*

In the first instance the injured player shall be entitled to wear any protective device prescribed by the Club doctor. If any opposing Club objects to the device it may record its objection with the President who shall promptly poll the Rules Committee for approval or otherwise.

c A glove from which all or part of the palm has been removed or cut to permit the use of the bare hand shall be considered illegal equipment and if any player wears such a glove in play a minor penalty shall be imposed on him.

NOTE *The Referee-in-Chief is specifically authorized to make a check of each team's equipment to ensure the compliance with this rule. He shall report his findings to the President for his disciplinary action.*

Rule 25 / Puck

a The puck shall be made of vulcanized rubber, or other approved material, one inch thick and three inches in diameter and shall weigh between five and a half ounces and six ounces. All pucks used in competition must be approved by the Rules Committee.

b The home team shall be responsible for providing an adequate supply of official pucks which shall be kept in a frozen condition. This supply of pucks shall be kept at the penalty bench under the control of one of the regular minor officials or a special attendant.

NOTE *As of June 9, 1980, pucks manufactured by the Viceroy Manufacturing Co., the In Glas Co Corporation, and Superior Fabricators Co. have been approved by the Rules Committee.*

NOTE TO SECTION THREE *A request for measurement of any equipment covered by this section shall be limited to one request by each Club during the course of any stoppage of play.*

The Referee may, at his own discretion, measure any equipment used for the first time in the game.

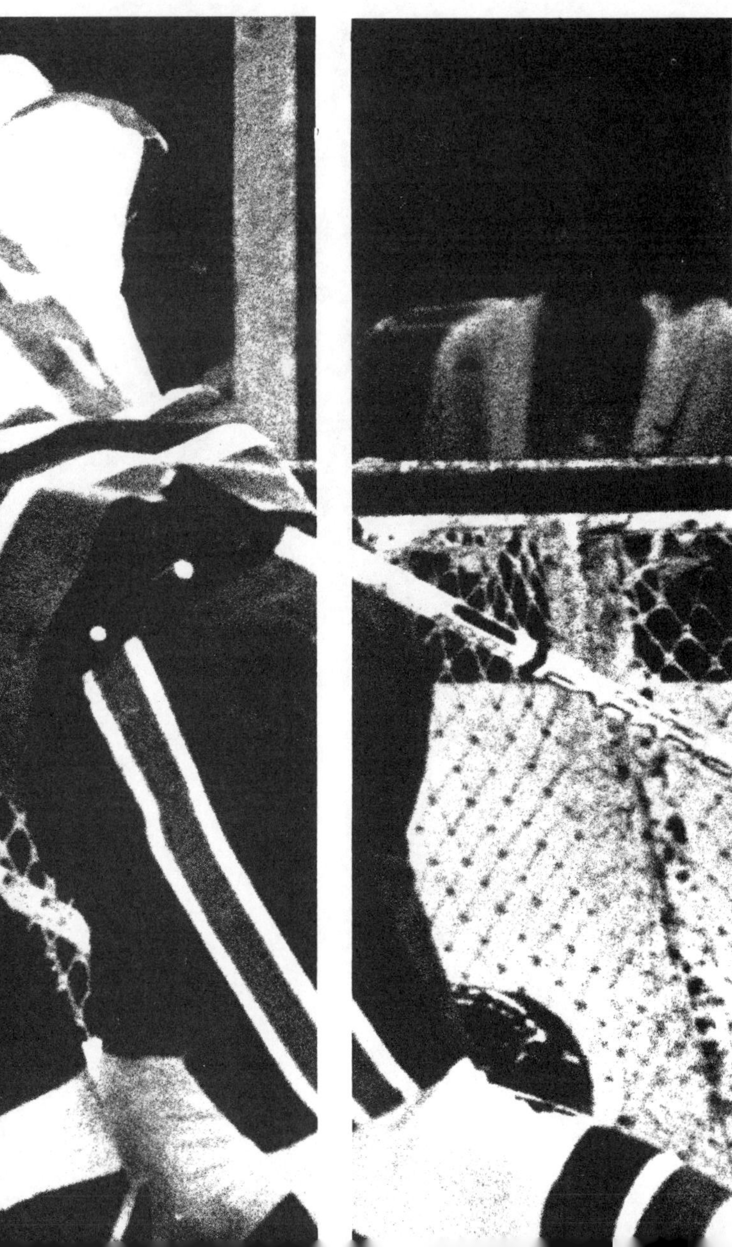

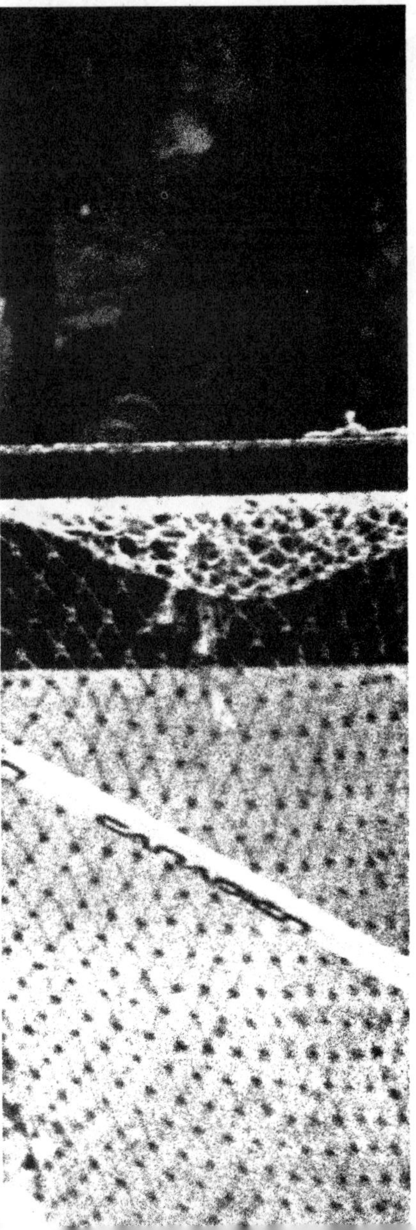

Rule 26 / Penalties

Penalties shall be actual playing time and shall be divided into the following classes:

1 Minor Penalties

2 Bench Minor Penalties

3 Major Penalties

4 Misconduct Penalties

5 Match Penalties

6 Penalty Shot.

Where coincident penalties are imposed on players of both teams the penalized players of the visiting team shall take their positions on the penalty bench first in the place designated for visiting players.

NOTE *When play is not actually in progress and an offense is committed by any player, the same penalty shall apply as though play were actually in progress.*

Rule 27 / Minor Penalties

a For a "MINOR PENALTY", any player, other than a goalkeeper, shall be ruled off the ice for two minutes during which time no substitute shall be permitted.

b A "BENCH MINOR" penalty involves the removal from the ice of one player of the team against which the penalty is awarded for a period of two minutes. Any player except a goalkeeper of the team may be designated to serve the penalty by the Manager or Coach through the playing Captain and such player shall take his place on the penalty bench promptly and serve the penalty as if it was a minor penalty imposed upon him.

c If while a team is "short-handed" by one or more minor or bench minor penalties the opposing team scores a goal, the first of such penalties shall automatically terminate.

NOTE *"Short-handed" means that the team must be below the numerical strength of its opponents on the ice at the time the goal is scored. The minor or bench minor penalty which terminates automatically is the one which causes the team scored against to be "short-handed". Thus coincident minor penalties to both teams do NOT cause either side to be "short-handed".*

This rule shall also apply when a goal is scored on a penalty shot.

When the minor penalties of two players of the same team terminate at the same time the Captain of that team shall designate to the Referee which of such players will return to the ice first and the Referee will instruct the Penalty Timekeeper accordingly.

When a player receives a major penalty and a minor penalty at the same time the major penalty shall be served first by the penalized player except under Rule 28 (c) in which case the minor penalty will be recorded and served first.

NOTE *This applies to the case where BOTH penalties are imposed on the SAME player. See also Note to Rule 33.*

d If while a team is short-handed by one penalty, coincident minor penalties of equal duration are imposed against a player of each team, then immediate substitution shall be made for such players.

Rule 28 / Major Penalties

a For the first "MAJOR PENALTY" in any one game, the offender, except the goalkeeper, shall be ruled off the ice for five minutes, during which time no substitute shall be permitted.

An automatic fine of fifty dollars ($50.00) shall also be added when a major penalty is imposed for any foul causing injury to the face or head of an opponent by means of a stick.

b For the third major penalty in the same game, to the same player, he shall be ruled off the ice for the balance of the playing time, but a substitute shall be permitted to replace the player so suspended after five minutes shall have elapsed. (Major penalty plus game misconduct penalty with automatic fine of one hundred dollars [$100.00].)

c When coincident major penalties or coincident penalties of equal duration, including a major penalty, are imposed against players of both teams, the penalized players shall all take their places on the penalty benches and such penalized players shall not leave the penalty bench until the first stoppage of play following the expiry of their respective penalties. Immediate substitutions shall be made for an equal number of major penalties or *coincident penalties of equal duration including a major penalty* to each team so penalized and the penalties of the players *for* which substitution have been made shall not be taken into account for the purpose of the delayed Rule 33.

Where it is required to determine which of the penalized players shall be designated to serve the delayed penalty under Rule 33 the penalized team shall have the right to make such designation not in conflict with Rule 27.

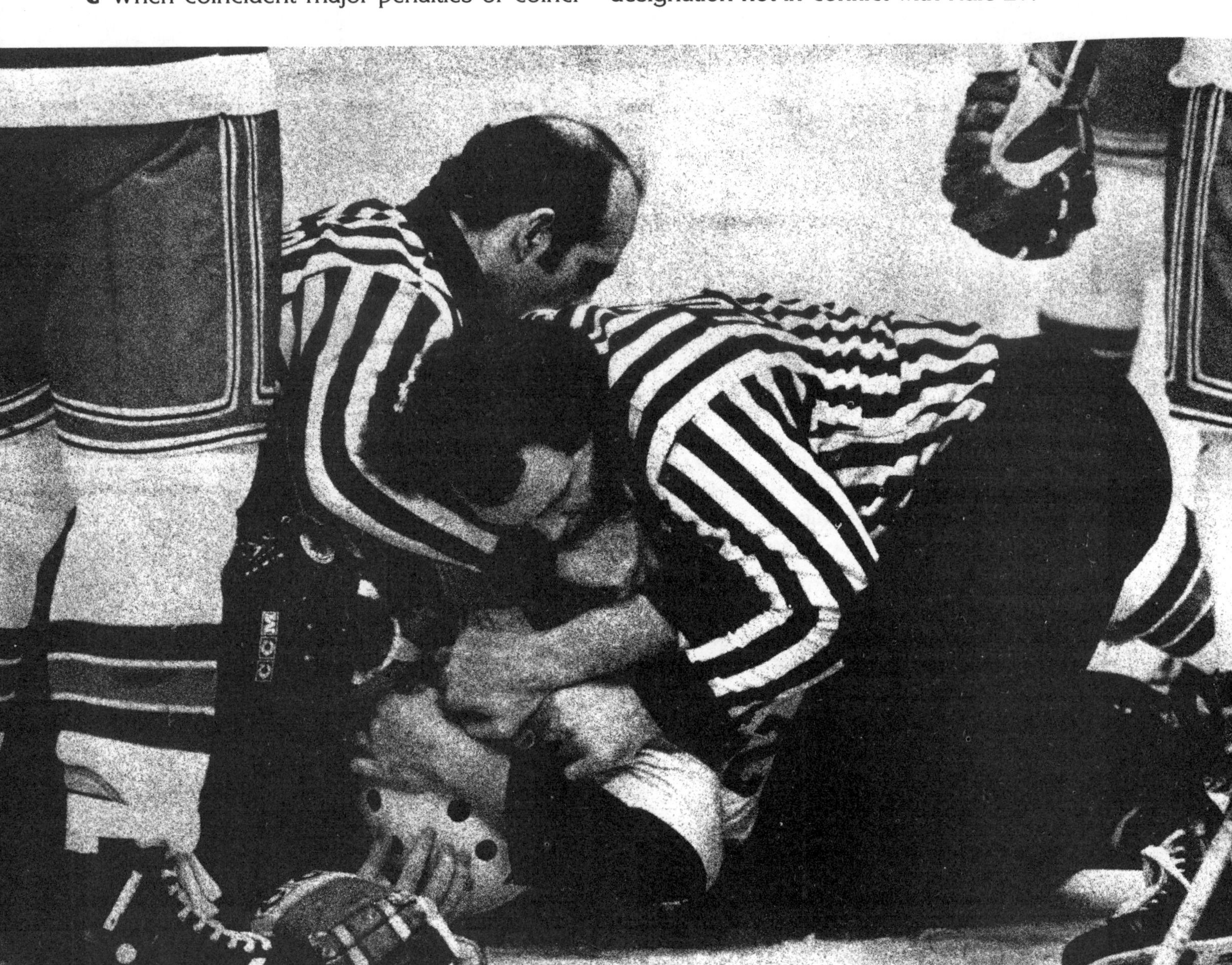

Rule 29 / Misconduct Penalties

a "MISCONDUCT" penalties to all players except the goalkeeper, involve removal from the game for a period of ten minutes each. A substitute player is permitted to immediately replace a player serving a misconduct penalty. A player whose misconduct penalty has expired shall remain in the penalty box until the next stoppage of play.

When a player receives a minor penalty and a misconduct penalty at the same time, the penalized team shall immediately put a substitute player on the penalty bench and he shall serve the minor penalty without change.

When a player receives a major penalty and a misconduct penalty at the same time, the penalized team shall place a substitute player on the penalty bench before the major penalty expires and no replacement for the penalized player shall be permitted to enter the game except from the penalty bench. Any violation of this provision shall be treated as an illegal substitution under Rule 18 calling for a bench minor penalty.

b A misconduct penalty imposed on any player at any time, shall be accompanied with an automatic fine of fifty dollars ($50.00).

c A "GAME MISCONDUCT" penalty involves the suspension of a player for the balance of the game but a substitute is permitted to replace immediately the player so removed. A player incurring a game misconduct penalty shall incur an automatic fine of one hundred dollars ($100.00) and the case shall be reported to the President who shall have full power to impose such further penalties by way of suspension or fine on the penalized player or any other player involved in the altercation.

d A Game Misconduct penalty shall be imposed on any player or goalkeeper who is the first to intervene in an altercation then in progress. This penalty is in addition to any other penalty incurred in the same incident.

e The Referee may impose a "GROSS MIS-CONDUCT" penalty on any player, Manager, Coach or Trainer who is guilty of gross misconduct of any kind. Any person incurring a "Gross Misconduct" penalty shall be suspended for the balance of the game and shall incur an automatic fine of one hundred dollars ($100) and the case shall be referred to the President of the League for further disciplinary action.

NOTE *For all "Game Misconduct" and "Gross Misconduct" penalties regardless of when imposed, a total of ten minutes shall be charged in the records against the offending player.*

f In regular League games, any player who incurs a total of three Game Misconduct penalties shall be suspended automatically for the next League game of his team. For each subsequent Game Misconduct penalty the automatic suspension shall be increased by one game. For each suspension of a player his Club shall be fined one thousand dollars ($1000).

In Play-off games any player who incurs a total of two Game Misconduct penalties shall be suspended automatically for the next Play-off game of his team. For each subsequent Game Misconduct penalty during the Play-offs the automatic suspension shall be increased by one game. For each suspension of a player during Play-offs his Club shall be fined one thousand dollars ($1000).

NOTE *Any Game Misconduct penalty for which a player has been assessed an automatic suspension or supplementary discipline in the form of game suspension(s) by the President shall NOT be taken into account when calculating the total number of offenses under this subsection.*

The automatic suspensions incurred under this subsection in respect to League games shall have no effect with respect to violations during Play-off games.

Rule 30 / Match Penalties

a A "MATCH" penalty involves the suspension of a player for the balance of the game, and the offender shall be ordered to the dressing room immediately. A substitute player is permitted to replace the penalized player after ten minutes playing time has elapsed when the penalty is imposed under Rule 49, and after five minutes actual playing time has elapsed when the penalty is imposed under Rule 44.

NOTE 1 *Regulations regarding additional penalties and substitutes are specifically covered in individual Rules 44, 49 and 64 any additional penalty shall be served by a player to be designated by the Manager or Coach of the offending team through the playing Captain such player to take his place in the penalty box immediately.*

For all "MATCH" penalties, regardless of when imposed, or prescribed additional penalties, a total of ten minutes shall be charged in the records against the offending player.

NOTE 2 *When coincident match penalties have been imposed under Rule 44, Rule 49 or Rule 64 to a player on both teams Rule 28 (c) covering coincident major penalties will be applicable with respect to player substitution.*

b A player incurring a match penalty shall incur an automatic fine of two hundred dollars ($200.00) and the case shall be investigated promptly by the President who shall have full power to impose such further penalty by way of suspension or fine on the penalized player or any other player involved in the altercation.

NOTE *The Referee is required to report all match penalties and the surrounding circumstances to the President of the League immediately following the game in which they occur.*

Rule 31 / Penalty Shot

a Any infraction of the rules which calls for a "Penalty Shot" shall be taken as follows:—

The Referee shall cause to be announced over the public address system the name of the player designated by him or selected by the team entitled to take the shot (as appropriate) and shall then place the puck on the center face-off spot and the player taking the shot will, on the instruction of the Referee, play the puck from there and shall attempt to score on the goalkeeper. The player taking the shot may carry the puck in any part of the Neutral Zone or his own Defending Zone but once the puck has crossed the Attacking Blue Line it must be kept in motion towards the opponent's goal line and once it is shot the play shall be considered complete. No goal can be scored on a rebound of any kind and any time the puck crosses the goal line the shot shall be considered complete.

Only a player designated as a Goalkeeper or Alternate Goalkeeper may defend against the penalty shot.

b The Goalkeeper must remain in his crease until the player taking the penalty shot has touched the puck and in the event of violation of this rule or any foul committed by a goalkeeper the Referee shall allow the shot to be taken and if the shot fails he shall permit the penalty shot to be taken over again.

The goalkeeper may attempt to stop the shot in any manner except by throwing his stick or any object, in which case a goal shall be awarded.

NOTE *See Rule 80.*

c In case where a penalty shot has been awarded under Rule 62 (g)—Interference, under Rule 66 (k)—for illegal entry into the game, under Rule 80 (a)—for throwing a stick and under Rule 83 (b)—for fouling from behind, the Referee shall designate the player who has been fouled as the player who shall take the penalty shot.

In cases where a penalty shot has been awarded under Rule 18 (b)—deliberate illegal substitution with insufficient playing time remaining or Rule 50 (c)—deliberately displacing goal post or Rule 53 (c)—falling on the puck in the crease or Rule 57 (d)—picking up the puck from the crease area—the penalty shot shall be taken by a player selected by the Captain of the non-offending team from the players on the ice at the time when the foul was committed. Such selection shall be reported to the Referee and cannot be changed.

If by reason of injury the player designated by the Referee to take the penalty shot is unable to do so within a reasonable time, the shot may be taken by a player selected by the Captain of the non-offending team from the players on the ice when the foul was committed. Such selection shall be reported to the Referee and cannot be changed.

d Should the player in respect to whom a penalty shot has been awarded himself commit a foul in connection with the same play or circumstances, either before or after the penalty shot penalty has been awarded, be designated to take the shot he shall first be permitted to do so before being sent to the penalty bench to serve the penalty except when such a penalty is for a game misconduct or match penalty in which case the penalty shot shall be taken by a player selected by the Captain of the non-offending team from the players on the ice at the time when the foul was committed.

If at the time a penalty shot is awarded the goalkeeper of the penalized team has been removed from the ice to substitute another player the goalkeeper shall be permitted to return to the ice before the penalty shot is taken.

e While the penalty shot is being taken, players of both sides shall withdraw to the sides of the rink and beyond the center red line.

f If, while the penalty shot is being taken, any player of the opposing team shall have by some action interfered with or distracted the player taking the shot and because of such action the shot should have failed, a second attempt shall be permitted and the Referee shall impose a misconduct penalty on the player so interfering or distracting.

g If a goal is scored from a penalty shot the puck shall be faced at center ice in the usual way. If a goal is not scored the puck shall be faced at either of the end face-off spots in the zone in which the penalty shot has been tried.

h Should a goal be scored from a penalty shot, a further penalty to the offending player shall not be applied unless the offense for which the penalty shot was awarded was such as to incur a major or match penalty or misconduct penalty, in which case the penalty prescribed for the particular offense, shall be imposed.

If the offense for which the penalty shot was awarded was such as would normally incur a minor penalty, then regardless of whether the penalty shot results in a goal or not, no further minor penalty shall be served.

i If the foul upon which the penalty shot is based occurs during actual playing time the penalty shot shall be awarded and taken immediately in the usual manner notwithstanding any delay occasioned by a slow whistle by the Referee to permit the play to be completed which delay results in the expiry of the regular playing time in any period.

The time required for the taking of a penalty shot shall not be included in the regular playing time of any overtime.

Rule 32 / Goalkeeper's Penalties

a A Goalkeeper shall not be sent to the penalty bench for an offense which incurs a minor penalty, but instead the minor penalty shall be served by another member of his team who was on the ice when the offense was committed, said player to be designated by the Manager or Coach of the offending team through the playing Captain and such substitute shall not be changed.

b Same as 32 (a) above except change "minor" to "major".

c Should a goalkeeper incur three major penalties in one game he shall be ruled off the ice for the balance of the playing time and his

place will be taken by a member of his own Club, or by a regular substitute goalkeeper who is available. (Major penalty plus game misconduct penalty and automatic fine of one hundred dollars [$100.00].)

d Should a goalkeeper on the ice incur a misconduct penalty this penalty shall be served by another member of his team who was on the ice when the offense was committed, said player to be designated by the Manager or Coach of the offending team through the Captain and, in addition, the goalkeeper shall be fined fifty dollars ($50.00).

e Should a goalkeeper incur a game misconduct penalty, his place then will be taken by a member of his own club, or by a regular substitute goalkeeper who is available, and such player will be allowed the goalkeeper's full equipment. In addition the goalkeeper shall be fined one hundred dollars ($100.00).

f Should a goalkeeper incur a match penalty, his place then will be taken by a member of his own club, or by a substitute goalkeeper who is available, and such player will be allowed the goalkeeper's equipment. However, any additional penalties as specifically called for by the individual rules covering match penalties, will apply, and the offending team shall be penalized accordingly; such additional penalty to be served by another member of the team on the ice at the time the offense was committed, said player to be designated by the Manager or Coach of the offending team through the Captain. (See Rules 44, 49 and 64).

g A Goalkeeper incurring a match penalty shall incur an automatic fine of two hundred dollars ($200.00) and the case shall be investigated promptly by the President who shall have full power to impose such further penalty by way of suspension or fine on the penalized goalkeeper or any other player in the altercation.

h A minor penalty shall be imposed on a goalkeeper who leaves the immediate vicinity of his crease during an altercation. In addition, he shall be subject to a fine of one hundred dollars ($100.00) and this incident shall be reported to the President for such further disciplinary action as may be required.

NOTE *All penalties imposed on goalkeeper regardless of who serves penalty or any substitution shall be charged in the records against the goalkeeper.*

i If a goalkeeper participates in the play in any manner when he is beyond the center red line a minor penalty shall be imposed upon him.

Rule 33 / Delayed Penalties

a If a third player of any team shall be penalized while two players of the same team are serving penalties, the penalty time of the third player shall not commence until the penalty time of one of the two players already penalized shall have elapsed. Nevertheless, the third player penalized must at once proceed to the penalty bench but may be replaced by a substitute

until such time as the penalty time of the penalized player shall commence.

b When any team shall have three players serving penalties at the same time and because of the delayed penalty rule, a substitute for the third offender is on the ice, none of the three penalized players on the penalty bench may return to the ice until play has stopped. When play has been stopped, the player whose full penalty has expired, may return to the play.

Provided however that the Penalty Timekeeper shall permit the return to the ice in the order of expiry of their penalties, of a player or players when by reason of the expiration of their penalties the penalized team is entitled to have more than four players on the ice.

c In the case of delayed penalties, the Referee shall instruct the Penalty Timekeeper that penalized players whose penalties have expired shall only be allowed to return to the ice when there is a stoppage of play.

When the penalties of two players of the same team will expire at the same time the Captain of that team will designate to the Referee which of such players will return to the ice first and the Referee will instruct the Penalty Timekeeper accordingly.

When a major and a minor penalty are imposed at the same time on players of the same team the Penalty Timekeeper shall record the minor as being the first of such penalties.

NOTE *This applies to the case where the two penalties are imposed on DIFFERENT players of the same team. See also Note to Rule 27.*

Rule 34 / Calling of Penalties

a Should an infraction of the rules which would call for a minor, major, misconduct, game misconduct or match penalty be committed by a player of the side in possession of the puck, the Referee shall immediately blow his whistle and give the penalties to the deserving players.

The resulting face-off shall be made at the place where the play was stopped unless the stoppage occurs in the Attacking Zone of the player penalized in which case the face-off shall be made at the nearest face-off spot in the Neutral Zone.

b Should an infraction of the rules which would call for a minor, major, misconduct, game misconduct or match penalty be committed by a player of the team not in possession of the puck, the Referee will blow his whistle and impose the penalty on the offending player upon completion of the play by the team in possession of the puck.

NOTE *There shall be no signal given by the Referee for a misconduct or Game Misconduct penalty under this section.*

The resulting face-off shall be made at the place where the play was stopped, unless during the period of a delayed whistle due to a foul by a player of the side NOT in possession, the side in possession ices the puck, shoots the puck so that it goes out of bounds or is unplayable then the face-off following the stoppage shall take place in the Neutral Zone near the Defending Blue Line of the team shooting the puck.

If the penalty or penalties to be imposed are minor penalties and a goal is scored on the play by the non-offending side the minor penalty or penalties shall not be imposed but major and match penalties shall be imposed in the normal manner regardless of whether a goal is scored or not.

NOTE 1 *"Completion of the play by the team in possession" in this rule means that the puck must have come into the possession and control of an opposing player or has been "frozen." This does not mean a rebound off the goalkeeper, the goal or the boards or any accidental contact with the body or equipment of an opposing player.*

NOTE 2 *If after the Referee has signalled a penalty but before the whistle has been blown the puck shall enter the goal of the non-offending team as the direct result of the action of a player of that team, the goal shall be allowed and the penalty signalled shall be imposed in the normal manner.*

If when a team is "short-handed" by reason of one or more minor or bench minor penalties the Referee signals a further minor penal-

ty or penalties against the "short-handed" team and a goal is scored by the non-offending side before the whistle is blown then the goal shall be allowed, the penalty or penalties signalled shall be washed out and the first of the minor penalties already being served shall automatically terminate under Rule 27 (c).

c Should the same offending player commit other fouls on the same play, either before or after the Referee has blown his whistle, the offending player shall serve such penalties consecutively.

Rule 34A / Supplementary Discipline

In addition to the automatic fines and suspensions imposed under these Rules, the President may, at his discretion, investigate any incident that occurs in connection with any Exhibition, League or Play-off game and may assess additional fines and/or suspensions for any offense committed during the course of a game or any aftermath thereof by a player, Trainer, Manager, Coach or Club Executive whether or not such offense has been penalized by the Referee.

Rule 34B / Suspensions Arising from Exhibition Games

Whenever suspensions are imposed as a result of infractions occurring during exhibition games, the President shall exercise his discretion in scheduling the suspensions to ensure that no team shall be short more players in any regular League game than it would have been had the infractions occurred in regular League games.

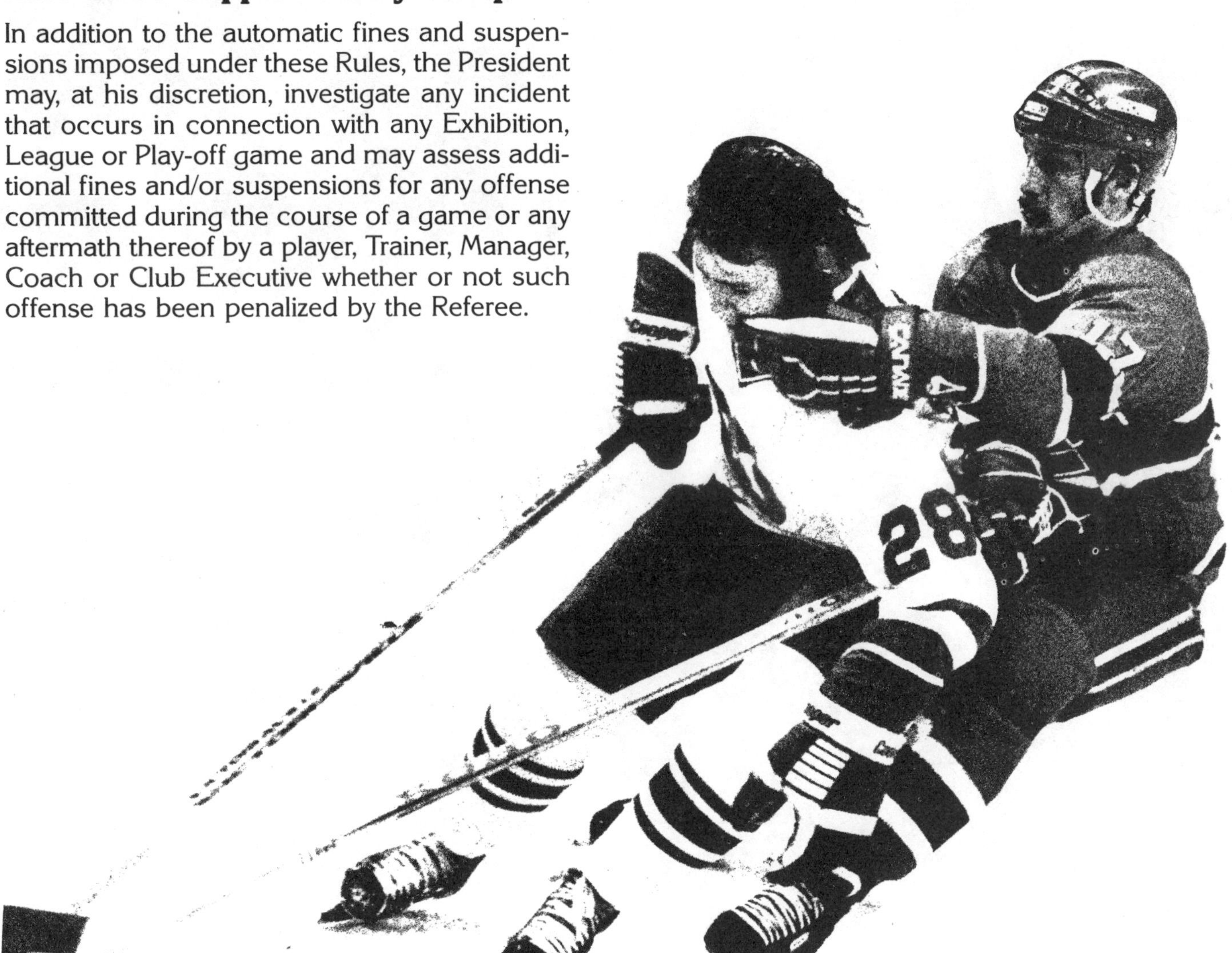

Officials

Rule 35 / Appointment of Officials

a The President shall appoint a Referee, two Linesmen, Game Timekeeper, Penalty Time-keeper, Official Scorer and two Goal Judges for each game.

b The President shall forward to all clubs a list of Referees, and Off-Ice Officials, all of whom must be treated with proper respect at all times during the season by all players and officials of clubs.

Rule 36 / Referee

a The REFEREE shall have general supervision of the game, and shall have full control of all game officials and players during the game, including stoppages; and in case of any dispute, his decision shall be final. The Referee shall remain on the ice at the conclusion of each period until all players have proceeded to their dressing rooms.

b All Referees and Linesmen shall be garbed in black trousers and official sweaters.

They shall be equipped with approved whistles and metal tape measures with minimum length of six feet.

c The Referee shall order the teams on the ice at the appointed time for the beginning of a game, and at the commencement of each period. If for any reason there be more than fifteen minutes' delay in the commencement of the game or any undue delay in resuming play after

the fifteen minute intervals between periods, the Referee shall state in his report to the President the cause of the delay, and the club or clubs which were at fault.

d It shall be his duty to see to it that all players are properly dressed, and that the approved regulation equipment is in use at all times during the game.

e The Referee shall, before starting the game, see that the appointed Game Timekeeper, Penalty Timekeeper, Official Scorer and Goal Judges are in their respective places, and satisfy himself that the timing and signaling equipment are in order.

f It shall be his duty to impose such penalties as are prescribed by the rules for infractions thereof, and he shall give the final decision in matters of disputed goals. The Referee may consult with the Linesmen or Goal Judge before making his decision.

g The Referee shall announce to the Official Scorer or Penalty Timekeeper all goals legally scored as well as penalties, and for what infractions such penalties are imposed.

The Referee shall cause to be announced over the public address system the reason for not allowing a goal every time the goal signal light is turned on in the course of play. This shall be done at the first stoppage of play regardless of any standard signal given by the Referee when the goal signal light was put on in error.

The referee shall report to the Official Scorer the name or number of the goal scorer but he shall *not* give any information or advice with respect to assists.

NOTE *The name of the scorer and any player entitled to an assist will be announced on the public address system. In the event that the Referee disallows a goal for any violation of the rules, he shall report the reason for disallowance to the Official Scorer who shall announce the Referee's decision correctly over the public address system.*

The infraction of the rules for which each penalty has been imposed will be announced correctly, as reported by the Referee, over the public address system. Where players of both teams are penalized on the same play, the penalty to the visiting player will be announced first.

Where a penalty is imposed by the Referee which calls for a mandatory or automatic fine, only the time portion of the penalty will be reported by the Referee to the Official Scorer and announced on the public address system, and the fine will be collected through the League office.

h The Referee shall see to it that players of opposing teams are separated on the penalty bench to prevent feuding.

i He shall not halt the game for any infractions of the rules concerning off-side play at the blue line, or center line or any violation of the "Icing the Puck" rule which shall be the function of the Linesman alone, unless the Linesman shall be prevented by some accident from doing so, in which case the duties of the Linesman shall be assumed by the Referee until play is stopped.

j Should a Referee accidentally leave the ice or receive an injury which incapacitates him from discharging his duties while play is in progress the game shall be automatically stopped.

k If, through misadventure or sickness, the Referee and Linesmen appointed are prevented from appearing, the Managers or Coaches of the two clubs shall agree on a Referee and Linesman. If they are unable to agree, they shall appoint a player from each side who shall act as Referee and Linesman; the player of the home club acting as Referee, and the player of the visiting club as Linesman.

l If the regularly appointed officials appear during the progress of the game, they shall at once replace the temporary officials.

m Should a Linesman appointed be unable to act at the last minute or through sickness or accident be unable to finish the game, the Referee shall have the power to appoint another, in his stead, if he deems it necessary, or if required to do so by the Manager or Coach of either of the competing teams.

n If, owing to illness or accident, the Referee is unable to continue to officiate, one of the Linesmen shall perform such duties as devolved upon the Referee during the balance of the game, the Linesman to be selected by the Referee.

o The Referee shall check Clubs' rosters and all players in uniform before signing reports of the game.

p The Referee shall report to the President promptly and in detail the circumstances of any of the following incidents:

1 When a stick or part thereof is thrown outside the playing area;

2 Every obscene gesture made by any person involved in the playing or conduct of the game whether as a participant or as an official of either team or of the League, which gesture he has personally observed or which has been brought to his attention by any game official;

3 When any player, trainer, coach or Club executive becomes involved in an altercation with a spectator.

4 Every infraction under Rule 77 (c) (slashing).

Rule 37 / Linesman

a The duty of the LINESMAN is to determine any infractions of the rules concerning off-side play at the blue line, or center line, or any violation of the "Icing the Puck" rule.

He shall stop the play when the puck goes outside the playing area and when it is interfered with by any ineligible person and when it is struck above the height of the shoulder and when the goal post has been displaced from its normal position. He shall stop the play for off-sides occurring on face-offs circles. He shall stop the play when there has been a premature substitution for a goalkeeper under Rule 18 (a) and for injured players under Rule 19 (f) and for a player batting the puck forward to a teammate under Rule 57 (e) and interference by spectators under Rule 63 (a).

b He shall face the puck at all times, except at the start of the game, at the beginning of each period and after a goal has been scored.

The Referee may call upon a Linesman to conduct a face-off at any time.

c He shall, when requested to do so by the Referee, give his version of any incident that may have taken place during the playing of the game.

d He shall not stop the play to impose any penalty except any violation of the Rule 18 (a) & (c)—Change of Players (too many men on the ice) and any violation of Rule 42 (k) (articles thrown on the ice from vicinity of players' or penalty bench) and Rule 46 (c) (stick thrown on ice from players' bench) and he shall report such violation to the Referee who shall impose a bench minor penalty against the offending team.

He shall report immediately to the Referee his version of the circumstances with respect to Rule 50 (c)—Delaying the game by deliberately displacing post from its normal position.

He shall report immediately to the Referee his version of any infraction of the rules constituting a major or match foul or Game Misconduct or any conduct calling for a bench minor penalty or misconduct penalty under these rules.

Rule 38 / Goal Judge

a There shall be one GOAL JUDGE at each goal. They shall not be members of either club engaged in a game, nor shall they be replaced during its progress, unless after the commencement of the game it becomes apparent that either Goal Judge, on account of partisanship or any other cause, is guilty of giving unjust decisions, when the Referee may appoint another Goal Judge to act in his stead.

b Goal Judges shall be stationed behind the goals, during the progress of play, in properly screened cages, so that there can be no interference with their activities; and they shall not change goals during the game.

c In the event of a goal being claimed, the Goal Judge of that goal shall decide whether or not the puck has passed between the goal posts and entirely over the goal line, his decision simply being "goal" or "no goal."

Rule 39 / Penalty Timekeeper

a The PENALTY TIMEKEEPER shall keep, on the official forms provided, a correct record of all penalties imposed by the officials including the names of the players penalized, the infractions penalized, the duration of each penalty and the time at which each penalty was imposed. He shall report in the Penalty Record each penalty shot awarded, the name of the player taking the shot and the result of the shot.

b The Penalty Timekeeper shall check and ensure that the time served by all penalized players is correct. He shall be responsible for the correct posting of penalties on the scoreboard at all times and shall promptly call to the attention of the Referee any discrepancy between the time recorded on the clock and the official correct time and he shall be responsible for making any adjustments ordered by the Referee.

He shall upon request, give a penalized player correct information as to the unexpired time of his penalty.

NOTE 1 *The infraction of the rules for which each penalty has been imposed will be announced twice over the public address system as reported by the Referee. Where players of both teams are penalized on the same play, the penalty to the visiting player will be announced first.*

NOTE 2 *Misconduct penalties and coincident major penalties should not be recorded on the timing device but such penalized players should be alerted and released at the first stoppage of play following the expiration of their penalties.*

c Upon the completion of each game, the Penalty Timekeeper shall complete and sign three copies of the Penalty Record to be distributed as quickly as possible to the following persons:—

1 One copy to the Official Scorer for transmission to the League President;

2 One copy to the visiting Coach or Manager;

3 One copy to the home Coach or Manager.

d The Referee-in-Chief shall be entitled to inspect, collect and forward to the League headquarters the actual work sheets used by the Penalty Timekeeper in any game.

Rule 40 / Official Scorer

a Before the start of the game, the Official Scorer shall obtain from the Manager or Coach of both teams a list of all eligible players and the starting line-up of each team which information shall be made known to the opposing team Manager or Coach before the start of play either personally or through the Referee.

The Official Scorer shall secure the names of the Captain, from the Manager or Coach at the time the line-ups are collected and will indicate those nominated by placing the letter "C" opposite their names on the Referee's Report of Match. All of this information shall be presented to the Referee for his signature at the completion of the game.

b The Official Scorer shall keep a record of the goals scored, the scorers, and players to whom assists have been credited, and shall indicate those players on the lists who have actually taken part in the game. He shall also record the time of entry into the game of any substitute goalkeeper. He shall record on the Official Score Sheet a notation where a goal is scored when the goalkeeper has been removed from the ice.

c The Official Scorer shall award the points for goals and assists and his decision shall be final. The awards of points for goals and assists shall be announced twice over the public address system and all changes in such awards shall also be announced in the same manner.

No requests for changes in any award of points shall be considered unless they are made at or before the conclusion of actual play in the game by the team Captain.

d At the conclusion of the game the Official Scorer shall complete and sign three copies of the Official Score Sheet for distribution as quickly as possible to the following persons:—

1 One copy to the League President;

2 One copy to the visiting Coach or Manager;

3 One copy to the home Coach or Manager.

e The Official Scorer shall also prepare the Official Report of Match for signature by the Referee and forward it to the League President together with the Official Score Sheet and the Penalty Record.

f The Official Scorer should be in an elevated position, well away from the Players' Benches, with house telephone communication to the Public Address Announcer.

Rule 41 / Game Timekeeper

a The Game Timekeeper shall record the time of starting and finishing of each period in the game and all playing time during the game.

b The Game Timekeeper shall signal the Referee and the competing teams for the start of the game and each succeeding period and the Referee shall start the play promptly in accordance with Rule 81.

To assist in assuring the prompt return to the ice of the teams and the officials the Game Timekeeper shall give a preliminary warning three minutes prior to the resumption of play in each period.

c If the rink is not equipped with an automatic gong or bell or siren or, if such device fails to function, the Game Timekeeper shall signal the end of each period by ringing a gong or bell or by blowing a whistle.

d He shall cause to be announced on the public address system at the nineteenth minute in each period that there is one minute remaining to be played in the period.

e In the event of any dispute regarding time, the matter shall be referred to the Referee for adjustment, and his decision shall be final.

Rule 41A / Statistician

a There shall be appointed for duty at every game played in the League a Statistician and such assistants or alternates as may be deemed necessary.

b The duty of the Statistician(s) is to correctly record on the official League forms supplied all of the data therein provided for concerning the performances of the individual players and the participating teams.

c These records shall be compiled and recorded in strict conformity with the instructions printed on the forms supplied and shall be completed as to totals where required and with such accuracy as to ensure that the data supplied is "in balance."

d At the conclusion of each game the Statistician shall sign and distribute three copies of the final and correct Statistician's Report to each of the following persons:—

1 One copy to the League President (through the Official Scorer if possible— otherwise by direct mail);

2 One copy to the visiting Coach or Manager;

3 One copy to the home Coach or Manager.

Rule 42 / Abuse of Officials and other Misconduct

NOTE *In the enforcement of this rule the Referee has, in many instances, the option of imposing a "misconduct penalty" or a "bench minor penalty." In principle the Referee is directed to impose a "bench minor penalty" in respect to the violations which occur on or in the immediate vicinity of the players' bench but off the playing surface, and in all cases affecting non-playing personnel or players. A "misconduct penalty" should be imposed for violations which occur on the playing surface or in the penalty bench area and where the penalized player is readily identifiable.*

a A misconduct penalty shall be imposed on any player who uses obscene, profane or abusive language to any person or who intentionally knocks or shoots the puck out of the reach of an official who is retrieving it or who deliberately throws any equipment out of the playing area.

b A minor penalty shall be assessed to any player who challenges or disputes the rulings of any official during a game. If the player persists in such challenge or dispute he shall be assessed a misconduct penalty and any further dispute will result in a Game Misconduct Penalty being assessed to the offending player.

c A misconduct penalty shall be imposed on any player or players who bang the boards with their sticks or other instruments any time.

In the event that the Coach, Trainer, Manager or Club Executive commits an infraction under this Rule a bench minor penalty shall be imposed.

d A bench minor penalty shall be imposed on the team of any penalized player who does not proceed directly and immediately to the penalty box and take his place on the penalty bench or to the dressing room when so ordered by the referee.

Where coincident penalties are imposed on players of both teams the penalized players of the visiting team shall take their positions on the penalty bench first in the place designated for visiting players, or where there is no special designation then on the bench farthest from the gate.

e Any player who (following a fight or other altercation in which he has been involved is broken up, and for which he is penalized) fails to proceed directly and immediately to the penalty bench; or who causes any delay by retrieving his equipment (gloves, sticks, etc. shall be delivered to him at the penalty bench by his teammates), shall incur an automatic fine of one hundred dollars ($100.00) in addition to all other penalties or fines incurred.

f Any player who persists in continuing or attempting to continue the fight or altercation after he has been ordered by the Referee to stop, or, who resists a Linesman in the discharge of his duties shall, at the discretion of the Referee, incur a Misconduct or a Game Misconduct penalty in addition to any penalties imposed.

g A misconduct penalty shall be imposed on any player who, after warning by the Referee, persists in any course of conduct (including threatening or abusive language or gestures or similar actions) designed to incite an opponent into incurring a penalty.

If, after the assessment of a Misconduct Penalty a player persists in any course of conduct for which he was previously assessed a Misconduct Penalty, he shall be assessed a Game Misconduct Penalty.

h In the case of any Club Executive, Manager, Coach or Trainer being guilty of such misconduct, he is to be removed from the bench by order of the Referee, and his case reported to the President for further action.

i If any Club Executive, Manager, Coach or Trainer is removed from the bench by order of the Referee, he must not sit near the bench of his club, nor in any way direct or attempt to direct the play of his club.

j A bench minor penalty shall be imposed against the offending team if any player, any Club Executive, Manager, Coach or Trainer uses obscene, profane or abusive language or gesture to any person or uses the name of any official coupled with any vociferous remarks.

k A bench minor penalty shall be imposed against the offending team if any player, Trainer, Coach, Manager or Club Executive in the vicinity of the players' bench or penalty bench throws anything on the ice during the progress of the game or during stoppage of play.

NOTE *The penalty provided under this rule is in addition to any penalty imposed under Rule 46 (c) "Broken Stick".*

l A bench minor penalty shall be imposed against the offending team if any player, Trainer, Coach, Manager or Club Executive interferes in any manner with any game official including Referee, Linesmen, Timekeepers or Goal Judges in the performance of their duties.

The Referee may assess further penalties under Rule 67 (Molesting Officials) if he deems them to be warranted.

m A misconduct penalty shall be imposed on any player or players who, except for the purpose of taking their positions on the penalty bench, enter or remain in the Referee's Crease while he is reporting to or consulting with any game official including Linesmen, Timekeeper, Penalty Timekeeper, Official Scorer or Announcer.

n A minor penalty shall be imposed on any player who is guilty of unsportsmanlike conduct including, but not limited to, hair-pulling, biting, grabbing hold of face mask, etc.

Rule 43 / Adjustment to Clothing and Equipment

a Play shall not be stopped nor the game delayed by reason of adjustments to clothing, equipment, shoes, skates or sticks.

For an infringement of this rule, a minor penalty shall be given.

b The onus of maintaining clothing and equipment in proper condition shall be upon the player. If adjustments are required, the player shall retire from the ice and play shall continue uninterruptedly with a substitute.

c No delay shall be permitted for the repair or adjustment of goalkeeper's equipment. If adjustments are required the goalkeeper will retire from the ice and his place will be taken by the substitute goalkeeper immediately and no warm-up will be permitted.

d For an infraction of this rule by a goalkeeper, a minor penalty shall be imposed.

Rule 44 / Attempt to Injure

a A match penalty shall be imposed on any player who deliberately attempts to injure an opponent and the circumstances shall be reported to the President for further action. A substitute for the penalized player shall be permitted at the end of the fifth minute.

b A Game Misconduct penalty shall be imposed on any player who deliberately attempts to injure an Official, Manager, Coach or Trainer in any manner and the circumstances shall be reported to the President for further action.

NOTE *The President, upon preliminary investigation indicating the probable imposition of supplementary disciplinary action, may order the immediate suspension of a player who has incurred a match penalty under this rule, pending the final determination of such supplementary disciplinary action.*

BOARDING
Pounding the closed fist of one hand into the open palm of the other hand.

Rule 45 / Board-Checking

a A minor or major penalty, at the discretion of the Referee based upon the degree of violence of the impact with the boards, shall be imposed on any player who bodychecks, cross-checks, elbows, charges or trips an opponent in such a manner that causes the opponent to be thrown violently into the boards.

NOTE *Any unnecessary contact with a player playing the puck on an obvious "icing" or "off-side" play which results in that player being knocked into the fence is "boarding" and must be penalized as such. In other instances where there is no contact with the fence it should be treated as "charging".*

"Rolling" an opponent (if he is the puck carrier) along the fence where he is endeavoring to go through too small an opening is not boarding. However, if the opponent is not the puck carrier, then such action should be penalized as boarding, charging, interference or if the arms or stick are employed it should be called holding or hooking.

b When a major penalty is imposed under this Rule for a foul resulting in injury to the face or head of an opponent an automatic fine of fifty dollars ($50) shall be imposed.

Rule 46 / Broken Stick

a A player without a stick may participate in the game. A player whose stick is broken may participate in the game provided he drops the broken portion. A minor penalty shall be imposed for an infraction of this rule.

NOTE *A broken stick is one which, in the opinion of the Referee, is unfit for normal play.*

b A goalkeeper may continue to play with a broken stick until stoppage of play or until he has been legally provided with a stick.

c A player whose stick is broken may not receive a stick thrown on the ice from any part of the rink but must obtain same at his players' bench. A goalkeeper whose stick is broken may not receive a stick thrown on the ice from any part of the rink but may receive a stick from a teammate without proceeding to his players' bench. A minor penalty shall be imposed on the player or goalkeeper receiving a stick illegally under this rule.

d A goalkeeper whose stick is broken or illegal may not go to the players' bench for a replacement but must receive his stick from a teammate.

For an infraction of this rule a minor penalty shall be imposed on the goalkeeper.

Rule 47 / Charging

a A minor or major penalty shall be imposed on a player who runs or jumps into or charges an opponent.

b When a major penalty is imposed under this rule for a foul, resulting in injury to the face or head of an opponent, an automatic fine of fifty dollars ($50.00) shall be imposed.

c A minor or major penalty shall be imposed on a player who charges a goalkeeper while the goalkeeper is within his goal crease.

NOTE *If more than two steps or strides are taken it shall be considered a charge.*

A goalkeeper is NOT "fair game" just because he is outside the goal crease area. A penalty for interference or charging (minor or major) should be called in every case where an opposing player makes unnecessary contact with a goalkeeper.

Likewise Referees should be alert to penalize goalkeepers for tripping, slashing or spearing in the vicinity of the goal.

CHARGING
Rotating clenched fists around one another in front of chest.

Rule 48 / Cross-Checking and Butt-Ending

a A minor or major penalty, at the discretion of the Referee, shall be imposed on a player who "cross-checks" an opponent.

b A major penalty shall be imposed on any player who "butt-ends" or attempts to "butt-end" an opponent.

NOTE *Attempt to "butt-end" shall include all cases where a "butt-end" gesture is made regardless whether body contact is made or not.*

c When a major penalty is imposed under this rule an automatic fine of fifty dollars ($50.00) shall also be imposed.

NOTE *Cross-check shall mean a check delivered with both hands on the stick and no part of the stick on the ice.*

Rule 49 / Deliberate Injury of Opponents

a A match penalty shall be imposed on a player who deliberately injures an opponent in any manner.

NOTE *Any player wearing tape or any other material on his hands who cuts or injures an opponent during an altercation shall receive a match penalty under this rule.*

b In addition to the match penalty, the Referee shall impose a fine of two hundred dollars ($200.00) on any player who deliberately injures another in any manner and the player shall be automatically suspended from further competition until the President has ruled on the issue.

c No substitute shall be permitted to take the place of the penalized player until ten minutes actual playing time shall have elapsed, from the time the penalty was imposed.

d A Game Misconduct penalty shall be imposed on any player who deliberately injures an Official, Manager, Coach or Trainer in any manner and the circumstances shall be reported to the President for further action.

Rule 50 / Delaying the Game

a A minor penalty shall be imposed on any player or goalkeeper who delays the game by deliberately shooting or batting the puck with his stick outside the playing area.

NOTE *This penalty shall apply also when a player or goalkeeper deliberately bats or shoots the puck with his stick outside the playing area after a stoppage of play.*

b A minor penalty shall be imposed on any player or goalkeeper who throws or deliberately bats the puck with his hand or stick outside the playing area.

c A minor penalty shall be imposed on any player (including goalkeeper) who delays the game by deliberately displacing a goal post from its normal position. The Referee or linesmen shall stop play immediately when a goal post has been displaced.

If the goal post is deliberately displaced by a goalkeeper or player during the course of a "break-away" a penalty shot will be awarded to the non-offending team, which shot shall be taken by the player last in possession of the puck.

NOTE *A player with a "break-away" is defined as a player in control of the puck with no opposition between him and the opposing goal and with a reasonable scoring opportunity.*

If by reason of insufficient time in the regular playing time or by reason of penalties already imposed the minor penalty awarded to a player for deliberately displacing his own goal post cannot be served in its entirety within the regular playing time of the game or at any time in overtime, a penalty shot shall be awarded against the offending team.

d A bench minor penalty shall be imposed upon any team which, after warning by the Referee to its Captain or designated substitute to place the correct number of players on the ice and commence play, fails to comply with the Referee's direction and thereby causes any delay by making additional substitutions, by persisting in having its players off-side, or in any other manner.

CROSS-CHECKING
A forward and backward motion
with both fists clenched extending from the chest.

Rule 51 / Elbowing, Kneeing and Head Butting

a A minor or major penalty, at the discretion of the Referee, shall be imposed on any player who uses his elbow or knee in such a manner as to in any way foul an opponent.

b When a major penalty is imposed under this rule for a foul resulting in an injury to an opponent an automatic fine of fifty dollars ($50.00) shall also be imposed.

c A match penalty shall be imposed on any player who deliberately "head-butts" or attempts to "head-butt" an opponent during an altercation and the circumstances shall be reported to the President for further action. A substitute shall be permitted at the end of the fifth minute. In the event there is an injury to an opponent resulting from the foul no substitute shall be permitted to take the place of the penalized player until ten minutes actual playing time shall be elapsed.

ELBOWING
Tapping the elbow of the "whistle hand" with the opposite hand.

KNEEING
Slapping the knee with palm of hand while keeping both skates on the ice.

Rule 52 / Face-Offs

a The puck shall be "faced-off" by the Referee or the Linesman dropping the puck on the ice between the sticks of the players "facing-off". Players facing-off will stand squarely facing their opponents' end of the rink approximately one stick length apart with the blade of their sticks on the ice.

When the face-off takes place in any of the end face-off circles the players taking part shall take their position so that they will have one skate on each side and clear of the line running through the face-off spot and with both feet behind him and clear of the line parallel to the goal line. The sticks of both players facing-off shall have the blade on the ice in contact with designated marking.

No other player shall be allowed to enter the face-off circle or come within fifteen feet of the players facing-off the puck, and must stand on side on all face-offs.

If a violation of this sub-section of this rule occurs the Referee or Linesman shall re-face the puck.

b If after warning by the Referee or Linesman either of the players fails to take his proper position for the face-off promptly, the official shall be entitled to face-off the puck notwithstanding such default.

c In the conduct of any face-off anywhere on the playing surface no player facing-off shall make any physical contact with his opponent's body by means of his own body or by his stick except in the course of playing the puck after the face-off has been completed.

For violation of this Rule the Referee shall impose a minor penalty or penalties on the player(s) whose action(s) caused the physical contact.

NOTE *"Conduct of any face-off" commences when the Referee designates the place of the face-off and he (or the Linesman) takes up his position to drop the puck.*

d If a player facing-off fails to take his proper position immediately when directed by the Official, the Official may order him replaced for that face-off by any teammate then on the ice.

No substitution of players shall be permitted until the face-off has been completed and play has been resumed except when a penalty is imposed which will affect the on-ice strength of either team.

e A second violation of any of the provisions of sub-section (a) hereof by the same team during the same face-off shall be penalized with a minor penalty to the player who commits the second violation of the rule.

f When an infringement of a rule has been committed or a stoppage of play has been caused by any player of the attacking side in the Attacking Zone the ensuing face-off shall be made in the Neutral Zone on the nearest face-off spot.

NOTE *This includes stoppage of play caused by player of attacking side shooting the puck on the back of the defending team's net without any intervening action by the defending team.*

g When an infringement of a rule has been committed by players of both sides in the play resulting in the stoppage, the ensuing face-off will be made at the place of such infringement or at the place where play is stopped.

h When stoppage occurs between the end face-off spots and near end of rink the puck shall be faced-off at the end face-off spot, on the side where the stoppage occurs unless otherwise expressly provided by these rules.

i No face-off shall be made within fifteen feet of the goal or sideboards.

j When a goal is illegally scored as a result of a puck being deflected directly from an official anywhere in the defending zone the resulting face-off shall be made at the end face-off spot in the defending zone.

k When the game is stopped for any reason not specifically covered in the official rules, the puck must be faced-off where it was last played.

l The whistle will not be blown by the official to start play. Playing time will commence from the instant the puck is faced-off and will stop when the whistle is blown.

Rule 53 / Falling on Puck

a A minor penalty shall be imposed on a player other than the goalkeeper who deliberately falls on or gathers a puck into his body.

NOTE *Any player who drops to his knees to block shots should not be penalized if the puck is shot under them or becomes lodged in their clothing or equipment but any use of the hands to make the puck unplayable should be penalized promptly.*

b A minor penalty shall be imposed on a goalkeeper who (when he is in his own goal crease) deliberately falls on or gathers the puck into his body or who holds or places the puck against any part of the goal in such a manner as to cause a stoppage of play unless he is actually being checked by an opponent.

NOTE *Refer to Rule 73 (c) for Rule governing freezing of puck by goalkeeper outside of his crease area.*

c No defending player, except the goalkeeper, will be permitted to fall on the puck or hold the puck or gather a puck into the body or hands when the puck is within the goal crease.

For infringement of this rule, play shall immediately be stopped and a penalty shot shall be ordered against the offending team, but no other penalty shall be given.

NOTE *This rule shall be interpreted so that a penalty shot will be awarded only when the puck is in the crease at the instant the offense occurs. However, in cases where the puck is outside the crease, Rule 53 (a) may still apply and a minor penalty may be imposed, even though no penalty shot is awarded.*

Rule 54 / Fisticuffs

a A major or a major and a Game Misconduct penalty, at the discretion of the Referee, shall be imposed on any player who starts fisticuffs.

b A minor penalty shall be imposed on a player who, having been struck, shall retaliate with a blow or attempted blow. However, at the discretion of the Referee a major or a double minor penalty or a Game Misconduct penalty may be imposed if such player continues the altercation.

NOTE 1 *It is the intent and purpose of this Rule that the Referee shall impose the "Major and Game Misconduct" penalty in all cases when the instigator or retaliator of the fight is the aggressor and is plainly doing so for the purpose of intimidation or punishment.*

NOTE 2 *The Referee is provided very wide latitude in the penalties which he may impose under this rule. This is done intentionally to enable him to differentiate between the obvious degrees of responsibility of the participants either for starting the fighting or persisting in continuing the fighting. The discretion provided should be exercised realistically.*

NOTE 3 *Referees are directed to employ every means provided by these Rules to stop "brawling" and should use this Rule and Rules 42 (e) and (f) for this purpose.*

c A Misconduct or Game Misconduct penalty shall be imposed on any player involved in fisticuffs off the playing surface or with another player who is off the playing surface.

d A Game Misconduct penalty, at the discretion of the Referee, shall be imposed on any player or goalkeeper who is the first to intervene in an altercation then in progress except when a match penalty is being imposed in the original altercation. This penalty is in addition to any other penalty incurred in the same incident.

e When a fight occurs all players not engaged in the altercation shall move to an area designated by the Referee upon his command. At the discretion of the Referee a ten-minute Misconduct penalty shall be assessed to any player or players who fail to move to the designated area when instructed to do so and/or to any player, including a goalkeeper, who removes his gloves and/or drops his stick during an altercation and who is not a participant in the original altercation. This penalty may be increased to a Game Misconduct penalty, if, in the judgment of the Referee, the player is the instigator of the subsequent altercation. This penalty is in addition to any other penalty incurred in the same incident.

Rule 55 / Goals and Assists

NOTE *It is the responsibility of the Official Scorer to award goals and assists, and his decision in this respect is final notwithstanding the report of the Referee or any other game official. Such awards shall be made or with-*

MISCONDUCT
Place both hands on hips.

held strictly in accordance with the provisions of this rule. Therefore, it is essential that the Official Scorer shall be thoroughly familiar with every aspect of this rule, be alert to observe all actions which could affect the making of an award and, above all, the awards must be made or withheld with absolute impartiality.

In case of an obvious error in awarding a goal or an assist which has been announced, it should be corrected promptly but changes should not be made in the offical scoring summary after the Referee has signed the Game Report.

a A goal shall be scored when the puck shall have been put between the goal posts by the stick of a player of the attacking side, from in front, and below the cross bar, and entirely across a red line, the width of the diameter of the goal posts drawn on the ice from one goal post to the other.

b A goal shall be scored if the puck is put into the goal in any way by a player of the defending side. The player of the attacking side who last played the puck shall be credited with the goal but no assist shall be awarded.

c If an attacking player kicks the puck and it is deflected into the net by any player of the defending side except the goalkeeper, the goal shall be allowed. The player who kicked the puck shall be credited with the goal but no assist shall be awarded.

d If the puck shall have been deflected into the goal from the shot of an attacking player by striking any part of the person of a player of the same side, a goal shall be allowed. The player who deflected the puck shall be credited with the goal. The goal shall not be allowed if the puck has been kicked, thrown or otherwise deliberately directed into the goal by any means other than a stick.

e If a goal is scored as a result of a puck being deflected directly into the net from an official the goal shall not be allowed.

f Should a player legally propel a puck into the goal crease of the opponent club and the puck should become loose and available to another player of the attacking side, a goal scored on the play shall be legal.

g Any goal scored, other than as covered by the official rules, shall not be allowed.

h A "goal" shall be credited in the scoring records to a player who shall have propelled the puck into the opponents' goal. Each "goal" shall count one point in the player's record.

i When a player scores a goal an "assist" shall be credited to the player or players taking part in the play immediately preceding the goal, but not more than two assists can be given on any goal. Each "assist" so credited shall count one point in the player's record.

j Only one point can be credited to any one player on a goal.

WASH-OUT
Both arms swung laterally across the body with palms down.
When used by the Referee it means goal disallowed.

Rule 56 / Gross Misconduct

Refer to Rule 29—Misconduct Penalty

Rule 57 / Handling Puck With Hands

a If a player, except the goalkeeper, closes his hand on the puck the play shall be stopped and a minor penalty shall be imposed on him. A goalkeeper who holds the puck with his hands for longer than three seconds shall be given a minor penalty.

b A goalkeeper must not deliberately hold the puck in any manner which in the opinion of the Referee causes a stoppage of play, nor throw the puck forward towards the opponents' goal, nor deliberately drop the puck into his pads or on to the goal net, nor deliberately pile up snow or obstacles at or near his net, that in the opinion of the Referee would tend to prevent the scoring of a goal.

NOTE *The object of this entire rule is to keep the puck in play continuously and any action taken by the goalkeeper which causes an unnecessary stoppage must be penalized without warning.*

c The penalty for infringement of this rule by the goalkeeper shall be a minor penalty.

NOTE *In the case of puck thrown forward by the goalkeeper being taken by an opponent, the Referee shall allow the resulting play to be completed, and if a goal is scored by the non-offending team, it shall be allowed and no penalty given; but if a goal is not scored, play shall be stopped and a minor penalty shall be imposed against the goalkeeper.*

d A minor penalty shall be imposed on a player except the goalkeeper who, while play is in progress, picks up the puck off the ice with his hand.

If a player, except the goalkeeper, while play is in progress, picks up the puck with his hand, from the ice in the goal crease area the play shall be stopped immediately and a penalty shot shall be awarded to the non-offending team.

e A player shall be permitted to stop or "bat" a puck in the air with his open hand, or push it along the ice with his hand, and the play shall not be stopped unless in the opinion of the Referee he has deliberately directed the puck to a teammate, in which case the play shall be stopped and the puck faced-off at the spot where the offense occurred.

NOTE *The object of this rule is to ensure continuous action and the Referee should NOT stop play unless he is satisfied that the directing of the puck to a teammate was in fact DELIBERATE.*

The puck may not be "batted" with the hand directly into the net at any time, but a goal shall be allowed when the puck has been legally "batted" or is deflected into the goal by a defending player except the goalkeeper.

Rule 58 / High Sticks

a The carrying of sticks above the normal height of the shoulder is prohibited, and a minor or major penalty may be imposed on a player violating this Rule, at the discretion of the Referee.

b A goal scored from a stick so carried shall not be allowed, except by a player of the defending team.

c When a player carries or holds any part of his stick above the height of his shoulder so that injury to the face or head of an opposing player results, the Referee shall have no alternative but to impose a major penalty on the offending player.

When a major penalty is imposed under this rule for foul resulting in injury to the face or head of an opponent, an automatic fine of fifty dollars ($50.00) shall also be imposed.

d Batting the puck above the normal height of the shoulders with the stick is prohibited and when it occurs there shall be a whistle and ensuing face-off at the spot where the offense occurred unless:

1 the puck is batted to an opponent in which case the play shall continue.

2 a player of the defending side shall bat the puck into his own goal in which case the goal shall be allowed.

NOTE *When player bats the puck to an opponent under sub-section 1 the Referee shall give the "wash-out" signal immediately. Otherwise he will stop the play.*

e When either team is below the numerical strength of its opponent and a player of the team of greater numerical strength causes a stoppage of play by striking the puck with his stick above the height of his shoulder, the resulting face-off shall be made at one of the end face-off spots adjacent to the goal of the team causing the stoppage.

HIGH-STICKING
Holding both fists, clenched, one above the other at the side of the head.

Rule 59 / Holding an Opponent

A minor penalty shall be imposed on a player who holds an opponent with hands or stick or in any other way.

Rule 60 / Hooking

a A minor penalty shall be imposed on player who impedes or seeks to impede the progress of an opponent by "hooking" with his stick.

b A major penalty shall be imposed on any player who injures an opponent by "hooking".

When a major penalty is imposed under this rule for a foul resulting in injury to the face or head of an opponent, an automatic fine of fifty dollars ($50.00) shall also be imposed.

NOTE *When a player is checking another in such a way that there is only stick-to-stick contact such action is NOT either hooking or holding.*

HOOKING
A tugging motion with both arms, as if pulling something toward the stomach.

HOLDING
Clasping the wrists of "the whistle hand" well in front of the chest.

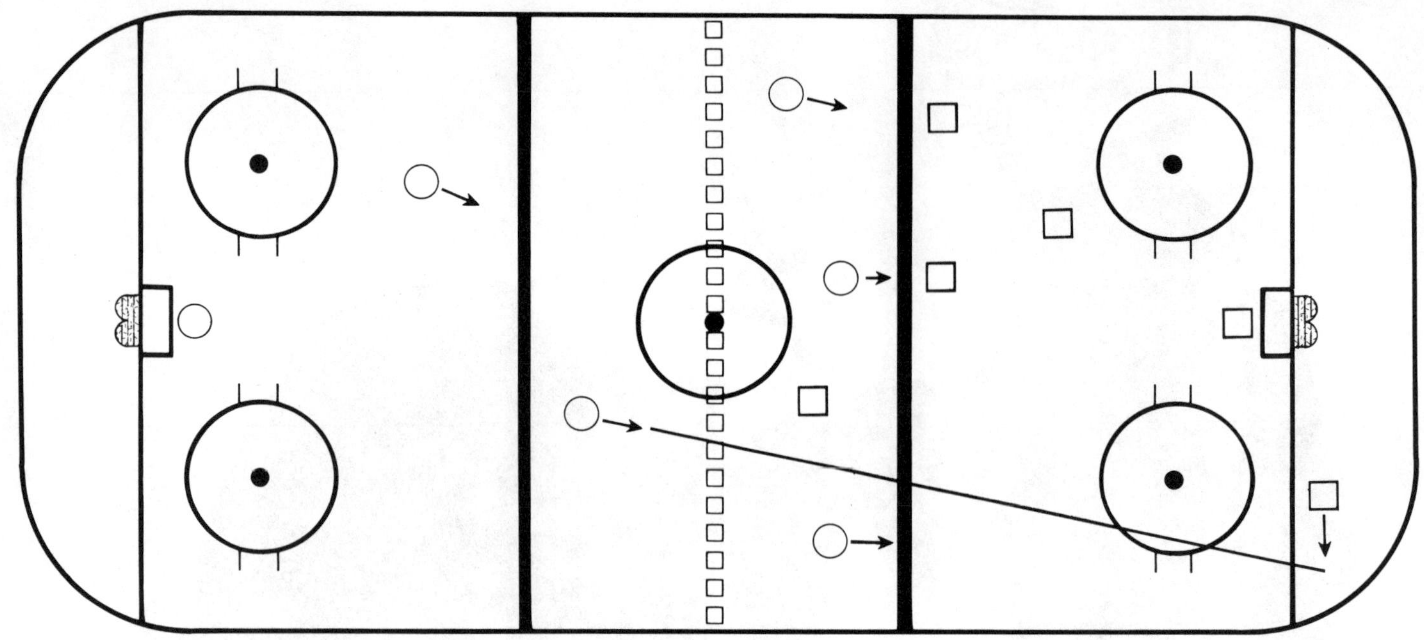

Rule 61 / Icing the Puck

a For the purpose of this rule, the center line will divide the ice into halves. Should any player of a team, equal or superior in numerical strength to the opposing team, shoot, bat, or deflect the puck from his own half of the ice, beyond the goal line of the opposing team, play shall be stopped and the puck faced off at the end face-off spot of the offending team, unless on the play the puck shall have entered the net of the opposing team, in which case the goal shall be allowed.

For the purpose of this rule the point of last contact with the puck by the team in possession shall be used to determine whether icing has occurred or not.

NOTE 1 *If during the period of a delayed whistle due to a foul by a player of the side NOT in possession, the side in possession "ices" the puck then the face-off following the stoppage of play shall take place in the Neutral zone near the Defending Blue Line of the team "icing" the puck.*

NOTE 2 *When a team is "short-handed" as the result of a penalty and the penalty is about to expire, the decision as to whether there has been an "icing" shall be determined at the instant the penalty expires. The action of the penalized player remaining in the penalty box will not alter the ruling.*

NOTE 3 *For the purpose of interpretation of this rule "Icing the Puck" is completed the instant the puck is touched first by a defending player (other than the goalkeeper) after it has crossed the Goal Line and if in the action of so touching the puck it is knocked or deflected into the net it is NO goal.*

NOTE 4 *When the puck is shot and rebounds from the body or stick of an opponent in his own half of the ice so as to cross the goal line of the player shooting it shall not be considered as "icing".*

NOTE 5 *Notwithstanding the provisions of this section concerning "batting" the puck in respect to the "icing the puck" rule, the provisions of the final paragraph of Rule 57 (e) apply and NO goal can be scored by batting the puck with the hand into the opponent's goal whether intended or not.*

NOTE 6 *If while the Linesman has signalled a slow whistle for a clean interception under Rule 71 (c), the player intercepting shoots or bats the puck beyond the opponent's goal line in such a manner as to constitute "icing the puck", the Linesman's "slow whistle" shall be considered exhausted the instant the puck crosses the blue line and "icing" shall be called in the usual manner.*

b If a player of the side shooting the puck down the ice who is on-side and eligible to play the puck does so before it is touched by an opposing player, the play shall continue and it shall not be considered a violation of this rule.

c If the puck was so shot by a player of a side below the numerical strength of the opposing team, play shall continue and the face-off shall not take place.

NOTE *If the team returns to full strength following a shot by one of its players, play shall continue and the face-off shall not take place.*

d If, however, the puck shall go beyond the goal line in the opposite half of the ice directly from either of the players while facing off, it shall not be considered a violation of the rule.

e If, in the opinion of the Linesman, a player of the opposing team excepting the goalkeeper is able to play the puck before it passes his goal line, but has not done so, the face-off shall not be allowed and play shall continue. If, in the opinion of the Referee, the defending side intentionally abstains from playing the puck promptly when they are in a position to do so, he shall stop the play and order the resulting face-off on the adjacent corner face-off spot nearest the goal of the team at fault.

NOTE *The purpose of this section is to enforce continuous action and both Referee and Linesmen should interpret and apply the rule to produce this result.*

f If the puck shall touch any part of a player of the opposing side or his skates or his stick, or if it passes through any part of the goal crease before it shall have reached his goal line, or shall have touched the goalkeeper or his skates or his stick at any time before or after crossing his goal line it shall not be considered as "icing the puck" and play shall continue.

NOTE *If the goaltender takes any action to dislodge the puck from back of the nets the icing shall be washed out.*

g If the Linesman shall have erred in calling an "icing the puck" infraction (regardless of whether either team is short-handed) the puck shall be faced on the center ice face-off spot.

ICING
Linesman's arms folded across the upper chest.

Rule 62 / Interference

a A minor penalty shall be imposed on a player who interferes with or impedes the progress of an opponent who is not in possession of the puck, or who deliberately knocks a stick out of an opponent's hand or who prevents a player who has dropped his stick or any other piece of equipment from regaining possession of it or who knocks or shoots any abandoned or broken stick or illegal puck or other debris towards an opposing puck carrier in a manner that could cause him to be distracted. (See also Rule 80 (a).)

NOTE *The last player to touch the puck—other than a goalkeeper—shall be considered the player in possession. In interpreting this rule the Referee should make sure which of the players is the one creating the interference—Often it is the action and movement of the attacking player which causes the interference since the defending players are entitled to "stand their ground" or "shadow" the attacking players. Players of the side in possession shall not be allowed to "run" deliberate interference for the puck carrier.*

b A minor penalty shall be imposed on any player on the players' bench or on the penalty bench who by means of his stick or his body interferes with the movements of the puck or of any opponent on the ice during the progress of play.

c A minor penalty shall be imposed on a player who, by means of his stick or his body, interferes with or impedes the movements of the goalkeeper by actual physical contact, while he is in his goal crease area unless the puck is already in that area.

d Unless the puck is in the goal crease area, a player of the attacking side may not stand on the goal crease line or in the goal crease or hold his stick in the goal crease area, and if the puck should enter the net while such condition prevails, a goal shall not be allowed, and the puck shall be faced in the neutral zone at face-off spot nearest the attacking zone of the offending team.

A minor penalty shall be imposed on any player of the attacking team who deliberately stands in the goal crease area.

e If a player of the attacking side has been physically interfered with by the action of any defending player so as to cause him to be in the goal crease, and the puck should enter the net while the player so interfered with is still within the goal crease, the "goal" shall be allowed.

f If when the goalkeeper has been removed from the ice any member of his team (including the goalkeeper) not legally on the ice, including the Manager, Coach or Trainer interferes by means of his body or stick or any other object with the movements of the puck or an opposing player, the Referee shall immediately award a goal to the non-offending team.

g When a player, in control of the puck in the opponent's side of the center red line, and having no other opponent to pass than the goalkeeper is interfered with by a stick or any part thereof or any other object thrown or shot by any member of the defending team including the Manager, Coach or Trainer, a penalty shot shall be awarded to the non-offending side.

NOTE *The attention of Referees is directed particularly to three types of offensive interference which should be penalized:*

1 *When the defending team secures possession of the puck in its own end and the other players of that team run interference for the puck carrier by forming a protective screen against forechecker;*

2 *When a player facing off obstructs his opposite number after the face-off when the opponent is not in possession of the puck;*

3 *When the puck carrier makes a drop pass and follows through so as to make bodily contact with an opposing player.*

Defensive interference consists of bodily contact with an opposing player who is not in possession of the puck.

INTERFERENCE
Crossed arms stationary in front
of chest with fists closed.

Rule 63 / Interference by/with Spectators

a In the event of a player being held or interfered with by a spectator, the Referee or Linesman shall blow the whistle and play shall be stopped, unless the team of the player interfered with is in possession of the puck at this time when the play shall be allowed to be completed before blowing the whistle, and the puck shall be faced at the spot where last played at time of stoppage.

b Any player who physically interferes with the spectators shall automatically incur a Gross Misconduct penalty and the Referee shall report all such infractions to the President who shall have full power to impose such further penalty as he shall deem appropriate.

c In the event that objects are thrown on the ice which interfere with the progress of the game the Referee shall blow the whistle and stop the play, and the puck shall be faced-off at the spot play is stopped.

NOTE *The Referee shall report to the President for disciplinary action, all cases in which a player becomes involved in an altercation with a spectator.*

Rule 64 / Kicking Player

A match penalty shall be imposed on any player who kicks or attempts to kick another player.

NOTE *Whether or not an injury occurs the Referee may, at his discretion, impose a ten minute time penalty under this rule.*

Rule 65 / Kicking Puck

Kicking the puck shall be permitted in all zones, but a goal may not be scored by the kick of an attacking player except if an attacking player kicks the puck and it is deflected into the net by any players of the defending side except the goalkeeper.

Rule 66 / Leaving Players' Bench or Penalty Bench

a No player may leave the players' bench or penalty bench at any time during an altercation, or for the purpose of starting an altercation. Substitutions made prior to the altercation shall be permitted provided the players so substituting do not enter the altercation.

b For violation of this rule a Double Minor penalty shall be imposed on the player of the team who was first to leave the players' bench or penalty bench during an altercation. If players of both teams leave their respective benches at the same time, the first identifiable player of each team to do so shall incur a Double Minor penalty. A Game Misconduct penalty shall also be imposed on any player who is penalized under this subsection and the Club of a player(s) incurring the Game Misconduct penalty shall incur a fine of one thousand dollars ($1000) for the first such incident, three thousand dollars ($3000) for the second such incident and five thousand dollars ($5000) for the third and each subsequent such incident.

c Any player (other than those dealt with under subsection (b) hereof) who leaves his players' bench during an altercation and is assessed any penalty for his actions, shall also incur an automatic Game Misconduct penalty.

d A player (other than those dealt with under subsection (b) hereof) who leaves his players' bench during an altercation, shall be subject to an automatic fine of one hundred dollars ($100.00) and the Referee shall report all such infractions to the President who shall have full power to impose such further penalty as he shall deem appropriate.

NOTE 1 *This automatic fine shall be imposed in addition to the normal penalties imposed for fouls committed by the player after he has left the players' bench.*

NOTE 2 *For the purpose of determining which player was first to leave his players' bench during altercation the Referee may consult with the Linesmen or Off-Ice Officials.*

e In regular League, Exhibition, and Play-off games any player who incurs a penalty under subsection (a) hereof (for leaving the players' bench or penalty bench first) shall be suspended automatically for the next three (3) regular League games of his team. For each subsequent violation by the same player the automatic suspension shall be increased by three (3) games.

Suspensions incurred during regular League play shall carry into the Play-offs.

f Except at the end of each period, or on expiration of penalty, no player may at any time leave the penalty bench.

g A penalized player who leaves the penalty bench before his penalty has expired, whether play is in progress or not, shall incur an additional minor penalty, after serving his unexpired penalty.

h Any penalized player leaving the penalty bench during stoppage of play and during an altercation shall incur a minor penalty plus a Game Misconduct penalty after serving his unexpired time.

i If a player leaves the penalty bench before his penalty is fully served, the Penalty Timekeeper shall note the time and signal the Referee who will immediately stop play.

j In the case of player returning to the ice before his time has expired through an error of the Penalty Timekeeper, he is not to serve an additional penalty, but must serve his unexpired time.

k If a player of an attacking side in possession of the puck shall be in such a position as to have no opposition between him and the opposing goalkeeper, and while in such position he shall be interfered with by a player of the opposing side who shall have illegally entered the game, the Referee shall impose a penalty shot against the side to which the offending player belongs.

l If the opposing goalkeeper has been removed and an attacking player in possession of the puck shall have no player of the defending team to pass and a stick or a part thereof or any other object is thrown or shot by an opposing player or the player is fouled from behind thereby being prevented from having a clear shot on an open goal, a goal shall be awarded against the offending team.

If when the opposing goalkeeper has been removed from the ice a player of the side attacking the unattended goal is interfered with by a player who shall have entered the game illegally, the Referee shall immediately award a goal to the non-offending team.

m If a Coach or Manager gets on the ice after the start of a period and before that period is ended the Referee shall impose a bench minor penalty against the team and report the incident to the President for disciplinary action.

n Any Club Executive or Manager committing the same offense, will be automatically fined two hundred dollars ($200.00).

o If a penalized player returns to the ice from the penalty bench before his penalty has expired by his own error or the error of the Penalty Timekeeper, any goal scored by his own team while he is illegally on the ice shall be disallowed, but all penalties imposed on either team shall be served as regular penalties.

p If a player shall illegally enter the game from his own players' bench or from the penalty bench, any goal scored by his own team while he is illegally on the ice shall be disallowed, but all penalties imposed against either team shall be served as regular penalties.

q A bench minor penalty shall be imposed on a team whose player(s) leave the players' bench for any purpose other than a change of players and when no altercation is in progress.

Rule 67 / Molesting Officials

a Any player who touches or holds a Referee, Linesman or any game official with his hand or his stick or trips or body-checks any of such officials, shall receive a ten-minute Misconduct Penalty or a Game Misconduct Penalty. The use of a substitute for the player so suspended shall be permitted.

b Any Club Executive, Manager, Coach or Trainer who holds or strikes an official, shall be automatically suspended from the game, ordered to the dressing room, and a substantial fine shall be imposed by the President.

Rule 68 / Obscene or Profane Language or Gestures

a Players shall not use obscene gestures on the ice or anywhere in the rink before, during or after the game. For a violation of this rule a game misconduct penalty shall be imposed and the Referee shall report the circumstances to the President of the League for further disciplinary action.

b Players shall not use profane language on the ice or anywhere in the rink before, during or after a game. For violation of this Rule, a Misconduct Penalty shall be imposed except when the violation occurs in the vicinity of the players' bench in which case a bench minor penalty shall be imposed.

NOTE *It is the responsibility of all game officials and all Club officials to send a confidential report to the President setting out the full details concerning the use of obscene gestures or language by any player, Coach or other official. The President shall take such further disciplinary action as he shall deem appropriate.*

c Club Executives, Managers, Coaches and Trainers shall not use obscene or profane language or gestures anywhere in the rink. For violation of this rule a bench minor penalty shall be imposed.

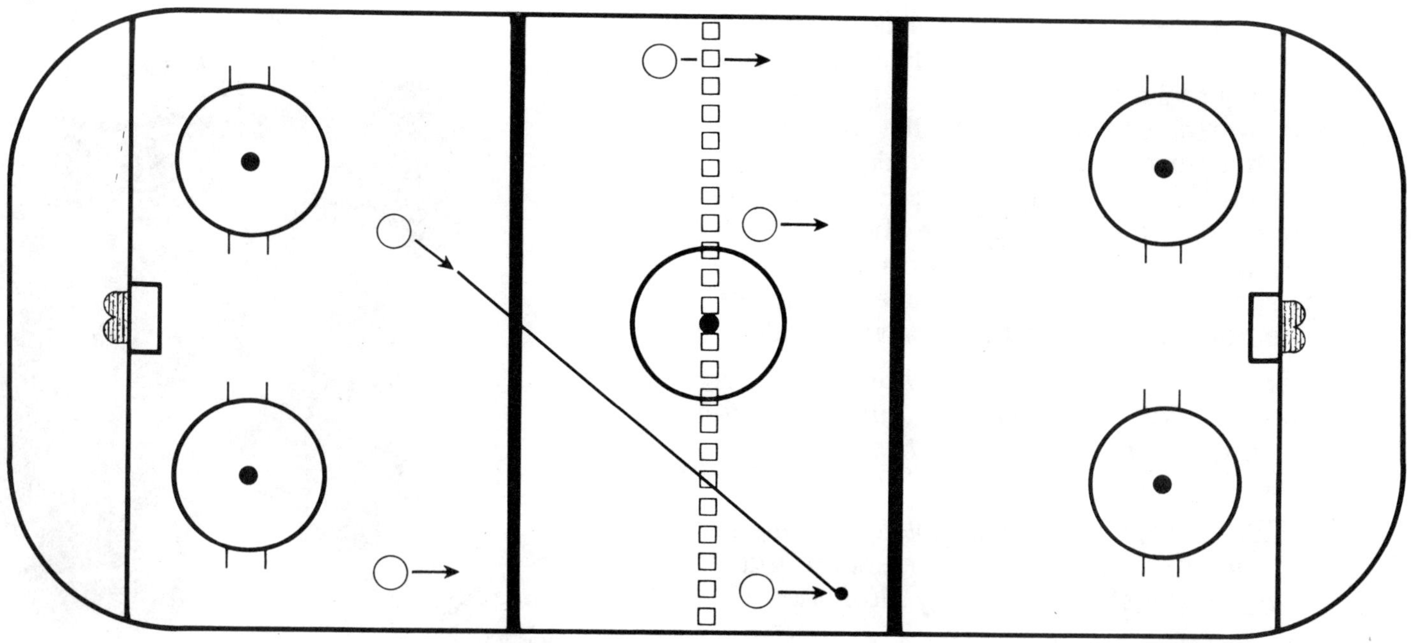

Rule 69 / Off-Sides

a The position of the player's skates and not that of his stick shall be the determining factor in all instances in deciding an "off-side." A player is off-side when both skates are completely over the outer edge of the determining center line or blue line involved in the play.

NOTE 1 *A player is "on-side" when "either" of his skates are in contact with or on his own side of the line at the instant the puck completely crosses the outer edge of that line regardless of the position of his stick.*

NOTE 2 *It should be noted that while the position of the player's skates is what determines whether a player is "off-side" nevertheless the question of "off-side" never arises until the puck has completely crossed the outer edge of the line at which time the decision is to be made.*

b If in the opinion of the Linesman an intentional off-side play has been made, the puck shall be faced-off at the end face-off spot in the defending zone of the offending team.

NOTE 3 *This rule does not apply to a team below the numerical strength of its opponent. In such cases the puck shall be faced-off at the spot from which the pass was made.*

NOTE 4 *An intentional off-side is one which is made for the purpose of securing a stoppage of play regardless of the reason, or where an off-side play is made under conditions where there is no possibility of completing a legal pass.*

c If the linesmen shall have erred in calling an off-side pass infraction (regardless of whether either team is shorthanded) the puck shall be faced on the center ice face-off spot.

Rule 70 / Passes

a The puck may be passed by any player to a player of the same side within any one of the three zones into which the ice is divided, but may not be passed forward from a player in one zone to a player of the same side in another zone, except by a player on the defending team, who may make and take forward passes from their own defending zone to the center line without incurring an off-side penalty. This "forward pass" from the Defending Zone must be completed by the pass receiver who is preceded by the puck across the center line, otherwise play shall be stopped and the face-off shall be at the point from which the pass was made.

NOTE 1 *The position of the puck (not the player's skates) shall be determining factor in deciding from which zone the pass was made.*

NOTE 2 *Passes may be completed legally at the center red line in exactly the same manner as passes at the attacking blue line.*

b Should the puck, having been passed, contact any part of the body, stick or skates of a player of the same side who is legally on-side, the pass shall be considered to have been completed.

c The player last touched by the puck shall be deemed to be in possession.

Rebounds off goalkeeper's pads or other equipment shall not be considered as a change of possession or the completion of the play by the team when applying Rule 34 (b).

d If a player in the Neutral Zone is preceded into the Attacking Zone by the puck passed from the Neutral Zone he shall be eligible to take possession of the puck anywhere in the Attacking Zone except when the "Icing the Puck" rule applies.

e If a player in the same zone from which a pass is made is preceded by the puck into succeeding zones he shall be eligible to take possession of the puck in that zone except where the "Icing the Puck" rule applies.

f If an attacking player passes the puck backward toward his own goal from the Attacking Zone, an opponent may play the puck anywhere regardless of whether he (the opponent) was in the same zone at the time the puck was passed or not. (*No "slow whistle."*)

Rule 71 / Preceding Puck into Attacking Zone

a Players of an attacking team must not precede the puck into the Attacking Zone.

b For violation of this rule, the play is stopped, and puck shall be faced-off in the Neutral Zone at face-off spot nearest the Attacking Zone of the offending team.

NOTE *A player actually controlling the puck who shall cross the line ahead of the puck, shall not be considered "off-side."*

c If however, notwithstanding the fact that a member of the attacking team shall have preceded the puck into the Attacking Zone, the puck be cleanly intercepted by a member of the defending team at or near the blue line, and be carried or passed by them into the Neutral Zone the "offside" shall be ignored and play permitted to continue.

(Officials will carry out this rule by means of the "slow whistle.")

d If a player legally carries or passes the puck back into his own Defending Zone while a player of the opposing team is in such Defending Zone, the "off-side" shall be ignored and play permitted to continue.

(No "slow whistle.")

Rule 72 / Puck Out of Bounds or Unplayable

a When the puck goes outside the playing area at either end, or either side of the rink or strikes any obstacles above the playing surface other than the boards, glass or wire it shall be faced-off from whence it was shot or deflected, unless otherwise expressly provided in these rules.

b When the puck becomes lodged in the netting on the outside of either goal so as to make it unplayable, or if it is frozen between opposing players intentionally or otherwise the Referee shall stop the play and face-off the puck at either of the adjacent face-off spots unless in the opinion of the Referee the stoppage was caused by a player of the attacking team, in which case the resulting face-off shall be conducted in the Neutral Zone.

NOTE *This includes stoppage of play caused by player of attacking side shooting the puck on to the back of the defending team's net without any intervening action by the defending team.*

The defending team and/or the attacking team may play the puck off the net at any time. However, should the puck remain on the net for longer than three seconds, play shall be stopped and the face-off shall take place in the end face-off zone except when the stoppage is caused by the attacking team, then the face-off shall take place on a face-off spot in the neutral zone.

c A minor penalty shall be imposed on a goalkeeper who deliberately drops the puck on the goal netting to cause a stoppage of play.

d If the puck comes to rest on top of the boards surrounding the playing area it shall be considered to be in play and may be played legally by hand or stick.

Rule 73 / Puck Must Be Kept in Motion

a The puck must at all times be kept in motion.

b Except to carry the puck behind its goal once, a side in possession of the puck in its own defense area shall always advance the puck towards the opposing goal, except if it shall be prevented from so doing by players of the opposing side.

For the first infraction of this rule play shall be stopped and a face-off shall be made at either end face-off spot adjacent to the goal of the team causing the stoppage, and the Referee shall warn the Captain or designated substitute of the offending team of the reason for the face-off. For a second violation by any player of the same team in the same period a minor penalty shall be imposed on the player violating the rule.

c A minor penalty shall be imposed on any player including the goalkeeper who holds, freezes or plays the puck with his stick, skates or body in such a manner as to deliberately cause a stoppage of play.

NOTE *With regard to a goalkeeper this rule applies outside of his goal crease only.*

d A player beyond his defense area shall not pass nor carry the puck backward into his Defense Zone for the purpose of delaying the game except when his team is below the numerical strength of the opponents on the ice.

e For an infringement of this rule, the face-off shall be at the nearest end face-off spot in the Defending Zone of the offending team.

Rule 74 / Puck Out of Sight and Illegal Puck

a Should a scramble take place, or a player accidentally fall on the puck, and the puck be out of the sight of the Referee, he shall immediately blow his whistle and stop the play. The puck shall then be "faced-off" at the point where the play was stopped, unless otherwise provided for in the rules.

b If, at any time while play is in progress a puck other than the one legally in play shall appear on the playing surface, the play shall not be stopped but shall continue with the legal puck until the play then in progress is completed by change of possession.

Rule 75 / Puck Striking Official

Play shall not be stopped if the puck touches an official anywhere on the rink, regardless of whether a team is shorthanded or not.

Rule 76 / Refusing to Start Play

a If, when both teams are on the ice, one team for any reason shall refuse to play when ordered to do so by the Referee, he shall warn the Captain and allow the team so refusing fifteen seconds within which to begin the game or resume play. If at the end of that time the team shall still refuse to play, the Referee shall impose a two-minute penalty on a player of the offending team to be designated by the Manager or Coach of that team, through the playing Captain; and should there be a repetition of the same incident the Referee shall notify the Manager or Coach that he has been fined the sum of two hundred dollars ($200.00). Should the offending team still refuse to play, the Referee shall have no alternative but to declare that the game be forfeited to the non-offending club, and the case shall be reported to the President for further action.

b If a team, when ordered to do so by the Referee, through its Club Executive, Manager or Coach, fails to go on the ice, and start play within five minutes, the Club Executive, Manager or Coach shall be fined five hundred dollars ($500.00); the game shall be forfeited, and the case shall be reported to the President for further action.

NOTE *The President of the League shall issue instructions pertaining to records, etc., of a forfeited game.*

Rule 77 / Slashing

a A minor or major penalty, at the discretion of the Referee, shall be imposed on any player who impedes or seeks to impede the progress of an opponent by "slashing" with his stick.

b A major penalty shall be imposed on any player who injures an opponent by slashing. When a major penalty is imposed under this rule for a foul resulting in injury to the face or head of an opponent, an automatic fine of fifty dollars ($50.00) shall also be imposed.

NOTE *Referees should penalize as "slashing" any player who swings his stick at any opposing player (whether in or out of range) without actually striking him or where a player on the pretext of playing the puck makes a wild swing at the puck with the object of intimidating an opponent.*

c Any player who swings his stick at another player in the course of any altercation shall be subject to a fine of not less than two hundred dollars ($200.00), with or without suspension, to be imposed by the President.

NOTE *The Referee shall impose the normal appropriate penalty provided in the other sections of this rule and shall in addition report promptly to the President all infractions under this section.*

SLASHING
A chopping motion with the edge of one hand across the opposite forearm.

KLAVANS
19

SPEARING
A jabbing motion with both hands thrust out in front of the body.

Rule 78 / Spearing

a A major penalty shall be imposed on a player who spears or attempts to spear an opponent.

NOTE *"Attempt to spear" shall include all cases where a spearing gesture is made regardless whether bodily contact is made or not.*

b In addition to the major penalty imposed under this rule an automatic fine of $50.00 will also be imposed.

NOTE 1 *"Spearing" shall mean stabbing an opponent with the point of the stick blade while the stick is being carried with one hand or both hands.*

NOTE 2 *Spearing may also be treated as a "deliberate attempt to injure" under Rule 44.*

Rule 79 / Start of Game and Periods

a The game shall be commenced at the time scheduled by a "face-off" in the center of the rink and shall be renewed promptly at the conclusion of each intermission in the same manner.

No delay shall be permitted by reason of any ceremony, exhibition, demonstration or presentation unless consented to reasonably in advance by the visiting team.

b Home clubs shall have the choice of goals to defend at the start of the game except where both players' benches are on the same side of the rink, in which case the home club shall start the game defending the goal nearest to its own bench. The teams shall change ends for each succeeding regular or overtime period.

c During the pre-game warm-up (which shall not exceed twenty minutes in duration) and before the commencement of play in any period each team shall confine its activity to its own end of the rink so as to leave clear an area thirty feet wide across the center of the Neutral Zone.

NOTE 1 *The Game Timekeeper shall be responsible for signalling the commencement and termination of the pre-game warm-up and any violation of this rule by the players shall be reported to the President by the Supervisor when in attendance at game.*

NOTE 2 *Players shall not be permitted to come on the ice during a stoppage in play or at the end of the first and second periods for the purpose of warming-up. The Referee will report any violation of this rule to the President for disciplinary action.*

d Fifteen minutes before the time scheduled for the start of the game both teams shall vacate the ice and proceed to their dressing rooms while the ice is being flooded. Both teams shall be signalled by the Game Timekeeper to return to the ice together in time for the scheduled start of the game.

e When a team fails to appear on the ice promptly without proper justification a fine shall be assessed against the offending team. The amount of the fine to be decided by the President.

Rule 80 / Throwing Stick

a When any player of the defending side or Manager, Coach or Trainer, deliberately throws or shoots a stick or any part thereof or any other object, at the puck in his Defending Zone, the Referee shall allow the play to be completed and if a goal is not scored a penalty shot shall be awarded to the non-offending side, which shot shall be taken by the player designated by the Referee as the player fouled.

If, however, the goal being unattended and the attacking player having no defending player to pass and having a chance to score on an "open net," a stick or part thereof or any other object, be thrown or shot by any member of the defending team, including the Manager, Coach or Trainer thereby preventing a shot on the "open net" a goal shall be awarded to the attacking side.

NOTE 1 *If the officials are unable to determine the person against whom the offense was made the offended team through the Captain shall designate the player on the ice at the time the offense was committed who will take the shot.*

NOTE 2 *For the purpose of this rule, an open net is defined as one from which a goal-keeper has been removed for an additional attacking player.*

b A major penalty shall be imposed on any player *on the ice* who throws his stick or any part thereof or any other object in the direction of the puck in any zone, except when such act has been penalized by the assessment of a penalty shot or the award of a goal.

NOTE *When a player discards the broken portion of a stick by tossing it to the side of the ice (and not over the boards) in such a way as will not interfere with play or opposing player, no penalty will be imposed for so doing.*

c A Misconduct or Game Misconduct penalty, at the discretion of the Referee, shall be imposed on a player who throws his stick or any part thereof outside the playing area. If the offense is committed in protest of an official's decision a minor penalty for unsportsmanlike conduct plus a Game Misconduct penalty shall be assessed to the offending player.

Rule 81 / Time of Match

a The time allowed for a game shall be three twenty-minute periods of actual play with a rest intermission between periods.

Play shall be resumed promptly following each intermission upon the expiry of fifteen minutes from the completion of play in the preceding period. A preliminary warning shall be given by the Game Timekeeper to the officials and to both teams three minutes prior to the resump-

tion of play in each period and the final warning shall be given in sufficient time to enable the teams to resume play promptly.

NOTE *For the purpose of keeping the spectators informed as to the time remaining during intermissions the Game Timekeeper will use the electric clock to record length of intermissions.*

b The team scoring the greatest number of goals during the three twenty-minute periods shall be the winner, and shall be credited with two points in the League standing.

c In the intervals between periods, the ice surface shall be flooded unless mutually agreed to the contrary.

d If any unusual delay occurs within five minutes of the end of the first or second periods the Referee may order the next regular intermission to be taken immediately and the balance of the period will be completed on the resumption of play with the teams defending the same goals, after which the teams will change ends and resume play of the ensuing period without delay.

NOTE *If a delay takes place with more than five minutes remaining in the first or second period, the Referee will order the next regular intermission to be taken immediately only when requested to do so by the Home Club.*

Rule 82 / Tied Games

a If, at the end of three (3) regular twenty-minute periods the score shall be tied, the teams will play an additional period of not more than five (5) minutes with the team scoring first being declared the winner. If, at the end of the overtime period, the score remains tied each team shall be credited with one point in the League standing.

NOTE *The overtime period will be commenced immediately following a two-minute rest period during which the players will remain on the ice. The teams will switch ends for the overtime period.*

b Special conditions for duration and number of periods of play-off games, shall be arranged by the Board of Governors.

TRIPPING
Strike the right leg with the right hand below the knee keeping both skates on the ice.

Rule 83 / Tripping

a A minor penalty shall be imposed on any player who shall place his stick, knee, foot, arm, hand or elbow in such a manner that it shall cause his opponent to trip or fall.

NOTE 1 *If in the opinion of the Referee a player is unquestionably hook-checking the puck and obtains possession of it, thereby tripping puck carrier, no penalty shall be imposed.*

NOTE 2 *Accidental trips occurring simultaneously with or after stoppage of play will not be penalized.*

b When a player, in control of the puck in the opponent's side of the center red line, and having no other opponent to pass than the goalkeeper, is tripped or otherwise fouled from behind thus preventing a reasonable scoring opportunity a penalty shot shall be awarded to the non-offending side. Nevertheless the Referee shall not stop the play until the attacking side has lost possession of the puck to the defending side.

NOTE *The intention of this rule is to restore a reasonable scoring opportunity which has been lost by reason of a foul from behind when the foul is committed in the opponent's side of the center red line.*

By "control of the puck" is meant the act of propelling the puck with the stick. If while it is being propelled the puck is touched by another player or his equipment or hits the goal or goes free the player shall no longer be considered to be "in control of the puck".

c If, when the opposing goalkeeper has been removed from the ice, a player in control of the puck is tripped or otherwise fouled with no opposition between him and the opposing goal, thus preventing a reasonable scoring opportunity, the Referee shall immediately stop the play and award a goal to the attacking team.

Rule 84 / Unnecessary Roughness

At the discretion of the Referee, a minor penalty or double minor penalty may be imposed on any player deemed guilty of unnecessary roughness.

Rule 85 / Time-Outs

Each team shall be permitted to take one time-out of thirty seconds duration during the course of regular time or over-time in the case of a play-off game and which must be taken during a normal stoppage of play. Any player designated by the Coach will indicate to the Referee that his team is exercising its option and the Referee will report the time-out to the Game Timekeeper who shall be responsible for signalling the termination of the time-out.

NOTE *All players including goalkeepers on the ice at the time of the time-out will be allowed to go to their respective benches. Only one time-out can be taken at a stoppage and no time-out will be allowed after a reasonable amount of time has elapsed during a normal stoppage of play.*

ROUGHING
A thrusting motion with the arm extending from the side.